P9-BIB-639

The
Wisdom of
John and Abigail
Adams

The Wisdom of John and Abigail Adams

MetroBooks

2002 MetroBooks

ISBN 1-58663-576-X

Text design by Kevin McGuinness

Printed and bound in the United States of America

02   03   04   05   06   MC   9   8   7   6   5   4   3   2   1

RRD-H

Contents

Foreword

HISTORY HAS FASHIONS; NOT SURPRISINGLY,
successive generations shift attention and admiration from one "Founding Father" to another.
Recently, John Adams (1735–1826) and Abigail
Smith Adams (1744–1818) have won their turn in
the spotlight. Historians are rediscovering the
complexity of John Adams's political thought and
his work as a prophet of American constitutionalism, and Abigail Adams's equally significant roles
as writer, observer of human affairs, and her husband's most trusted political advisor. And millions
find their humanity, humor, and profundity immensely appealing.

This book offers an introduction to the wisdom
of John and Abigail Adams. Drawing on the millions of words penned by these two articulate and
energetic people, it seeks to give a sense of the
ideas and values that mattered to them, the ways
in which they confronted their turbulent and exciting era and sought to make sense of it.

John Adams knew that he would be overshadowed by George Washington, Thomas Jefferson, and Benjamin Franklin. Not a commanding figure of the battlefield, as Washington was, nor the writer of the Revolution's classic statement of American values, as Jefferson was, nor a wide-ranging, genial sage, as Franklin was — still Adams has many virtues and achievements worth the attention of posterity.

Adams excelled in crafting legal and constitutional arguments, in sifting the amassed wisdom of Western civilization about politics and governance — in short, in the tasks of lawgiving. In an early pamphlet, he even dubbed God "the great Legislator of the universe." In the First (1774) and Second (1775-1776) Continental Congresses, he was a bulwark of resistance to what he deemed unconstitutional British policies; after Lexington and Concord, he was an uncompromising advocate of independence — the linchpin of that cause until Congress declared American independence.

At the same time, with energy and enthusiasm, he threw himself into guiding his fellow citizens to devise new forms of government to replace their colonial frameworks. Revolutions succeed when they build as well as pull down, and Adams deserves much of the credit for the Revolution's constructive achievements. His devotion to ideas of balanced government spurred him to write one of the greatest pamphlets in American constitutional thought, *Thoughts on Government* (1776), which for eloquence and cogency matches Thomas Paine's more influential *Common Sense* (1776). Three years later, he took the lead in drafting a new constitution for his native Massachusetts that, after its adoption in 1780, shaped all later American experiments in government.

Adams was also one of the first and most versatile American diplomats — though his blunt honesty hobbled his efforts and alienated his fellow envoy Benjamin Franklin. Nonetheless, in 1782-1783 Adams, Franklin, and John Jay negotiated the Treaty of Paris, which ended the war, won British recognition of American independence, and doubled the size of the new nation. Thereafter, Adams first sought to negotiate commercial treaties with European powers and then served as American Minister to Great Britain. While abroad, he wrote a three-volume treatise on comparative constitutional government, *A Defence of the Constitutions of Government of the United States* . . . (1787-1788), which many Americans read as an endorsement of kingly government. Adams's skeptical view of the French Revolution, which other Americans hailed as a continuation of their own revolution, only made things worse for him.

Adams spent eight unhappy years as first vice president of the United States (1789-1797), languishing in Washington's shadow, and four years (1797-1801) as second president of the United States. His presidency was turbulent and difficult; he faced a Cabinet filled with appointees he had inherited from Washington (they did not respect him and took their lead from former Treasury Secretary Alexander Hamilton) and a hostile French nation. When in 1798 the XYZ Affair touched off an undeclared naval war with France, Congress enacted and Adams signed into law the Alien and Sedition Acts — his administration's most criticized feature. Adams's foes (including his former friend Thomas Jefferson) saw these statutes as a machine for choking American liberty. When in 1800 Adams decided to seek peace with France, he split his own Federalist party; the Republicans won the presidency, and Adams became the first president defeated for re-election. He retired to his home in Quincy, Massachusetts, where he spent the last 25 years of his life, reading, writing, and reflecting.

By his side throughout his career was his wife, the redoubtable Abigail Adams. The daughter of two leading families (the Quincys and the

Smiths), she had received little formal schooling
and no college education (no woman did in this
period), but she had a powerful mind and a pronounced interest in educating herself and observ-
ing the world around her. She was an ideal
companion for John Adams, who admired her intelligence and character. When John Adams
"turned politician," his many journeys in America
and Europe made Abigail's life difficult; with
courage and skill she tended the family farm,
managed their finances, and raised several sons
and daughters, but could not contain her unhap-
piness with her husband's absences from home.
When he was named American Minister to Great
Britain, she finally joined him in Europe, and
thereafter, in all his offices, she was his chief con-
fidante and advisor.

John and Abigail Adams naturally resorted to
pen and paper to sort out their feelings, to assess
their lives, to make sense of the world and their
place in it. They left thousands of pages of letters,
diaries, and other writings, most of them still
awaiting publication. These writings are among
the greatest treasures of American literature —
including John Adams's diary and autobiography,
the correspondence between John and Abigail,
and John Adams's brilliant exchanges of letters
with Benjamin Rush and Thomas Jefferson. The

Massachusetts Historical Society's ongoing project with Harvard University Press, the Adams Papers, promises to make these writings generally available — but that project will take decades, perhaps, to be completed. Until then, various selected volumes (a list of some of the best appears at the end of this book) whet our appetites for more of the wisdom of John and Abigail Adams.

—R. B. Bernstein

NEW YORK LAW SCHOOL

JANUARY 2002

American Revolution

WE FURTHER RECOMMEND THE MOST CLEAR
and explicit assertion and vindication of our rights
and liberties to be entered on the public records,
that the world may know, in the present and all
future generations, that we have a clear knowledge and a just sense of them, and, with submis-
sion to Divine Providence, that we never can
be slaves.

> —**John Adams,** "Instructions of the
> Town of Braintree to their
> Representatives," 1765

LET US DARE TO READ, THINK, SPEAK, AND
write. Let every order and degree among the

people rouse their attention and animate their resolution. Let them all become attentive to the grounds and principles of government, ecclesiastical and civil. Let us study the law of nature; search into the spirit of the British constitution; read the histories of ancient ages; contemplate the great examples of Greece and Rome; set before us the conduct of our own British ancestors, who have defended for us the inherent rights of mankind against foreign and domestic tyrants and usurpers, against arbitrary kings and cruel priests, in short, against the gates of earth and hell.

> —**John Adams**, "A Dissertation on the Canon and Feudal Law," 1765

THE TEA THAT BAINFUL WEED IS ARRIVED. THE flame is kindled and like Lightening it catches from Soul to Soul. Great will be the devastation if not timely quenched or allayed by some more Lenient Measures. . . . Altho the mind is shocked at the Thought of sheding Humane Blood, more Especially the Blood of our countrymen, and a civil War is of all Wars, the most dreadfull, Such is the present State that prevails, that if once they are made desperate Many, very Many of our

Heroes will spend their lives in the cause, With the Speech of Cato in their Mouths, "What a pitty it is, that we can dye but once to save our Country."

> —**Abigail Adams** to Mercy Otis Warren,
> 5 DECEMBER 1773

IN ONE WORD, IF PUBLIC PRINCIPLES, AND motives, and arguments were alone to determine this dispute between the two countries, it might be settled forever in a few hours; but the everlasting clamors of prejudice, passion, and private interest drown every consideration of that sort, and are precipitating us into a civil war.

> —**John Adams,** *Novanglus,*
> 1774–1775

[IN THE FIRST CONTINENTAL CONGRESS] Business is drawn and spun out to an immeasurable Length. I believe if it was moved and seconded that We should come to a Resolution that Three and two make five We should be entertained with Logick and Rhetorick, Law, History, Politicks and Mathematicks, concerning the Subject for two whole Days, and then We should pass the Resolution unanimously in the Affirmative.

—**John Adams** to Abigail Adams,
9 OCTOBER 1774

A GOVERNMENT OF MORE STABILITY IS MUCH wanted in this colony, and they are to receive it from the Hands of the Congress, and since I have begun with Maxims of State I will add an other viz. that a people may let a king fall, yet still remain a people, but if a king let his people slip from him, he is no longer a king. And as this is most certainly our case, why not proclaim to the World in decisive terms your own importance? Shall we not be dispiced by foreign powers for hesitateing so long at a word?

—**Abigail Adams** to John Adams,
7 MAY 1776

YESTERDAY THE GREATEST QUESTION WAS
decided, which ever was debated in America, and
a greater perhaps, never was or will be decided
among Men. . . . It is the Will of Heaven, that the
two Countries should be sundered forever. It may
be the Will of Heaven that America shall suffer
Calamities still more wasting and Distresses yet
more dreadful. If this is to be the Case, it will
have this good Effect, at least: it will inspire Us
with many Virtues, which We have not, and cor-
rect many Errors, Follies, and Vices, which
threaten to disturb, dishonour, and destroy Us.
The Furnace of Affliction produces Refinement,
in States as well as Individuals. And the new
Governments we are assuming, in every Part, will
require a Purification from our Vices, and an
Augmentation of our Virtues or they will be no
Blessings. The People will have unbounded
Power. And the People are extreamly addicted to
Corruption and Venality, as well as the Great. I
am not without Apprehensions from this Quarter.
But I must submit all my Hopes and Fears, to an
overruling Providence, in which, unfashionable as
the Faith may be, I firmly believe.

> —**John Adams** to Abigail Adams,
> 3 JULY 1776

THE SECOND DAY OF JULY 1776, WILL BE THE most memorable Epocha, in the History of America. — I am apt to believe that it will be celebrated, by succeeding Generations, as the great anniversary Festival. It ought to be commemorated, as the Day of Deliverance by solemn Acts of Devotion to God Almighty. It ought to be solemnized with Pomp and Parade, with Shews, Games, Sports, Guns, Bells, Bonfires and Illuminations from one End of this Continent to the other from this Time forward forever more.

You will think me transported with Enthusiasm but I am not. — I am well aware of the Toil and Blood and Treasure, that it will cost Us to maintain this Declaration, and support and defend these States. — Yet through all the Gloom I can see the Rays of ravishing Light and Glory. I can see that the End is more than worth all the Means. And that Posterity will tryumph in that Days Transaction, even altho We should rue it, which I trust in God We shall not.

> —**John Adams** to Abigail Adams,
> 3 JULY 1776

POSTERITY! YOU WILL NEVER KNOW, HOW MUCH it cost the present Generation, to preserve your Freedom! I hope you will make a good Use of it. If you do not, I shall repent in Heaven, that I ever took half the Pains to preserve it.

> —**John Adams** to Abigail Adams,
>   26 APRIL 1777

AS TO THE HISTORY OF THE REVOLUTION, MY Ideas may be peculiar, perhaps singular. What do We Mean by the Revolution? The War? That was no part of the Revolution. It was only an Effect and Consequence of it. The Revolution was in the Minds of the People, and this was effected, from 1761 to 1775, in the course of fifteen Years before a drop of blood was drawn at Lexington. The Records of thirteen Legislatures, the Pamphlets, Newspapers in all the Colonies ought to be consulted, during that Period, to ascertain the Steps by which the public Opinion was enlightened and informed concerning the authority of Parliament over the Colonies.

> —**John Adams** to Thomas Jefferson,
>   24 AUGUST 1815

Constitutions and Constitution-Making

[I]F WE SEPERATE FROM BRITTAIN, WHAT CODE of Laws will be established. How shall we be governed so as to retain our Liberties? Can any government be free which is not administered by general stated Laws? Who shall frame these Laws? Who will give them force and energy?

—**Abigail Adams** to John Adams,
27 NOVEMBER 1775

[A]S THE DIVINE SCIENCE OF POLITICS IS THE science of social happiness, and the blessings of society depend entirely on the constitutions of government, which are generally institutions that last for many generations, there can be no employment more agreeable to a benevolent mind than a research after the best.

> —**John Adams,** *Thoughts on Government,*
> PHILADELPHIA, 1776

NOTHING IS MORE CERTAIN, FROM THE HISTORY of nations and nature of man, than that some forms of government are better fitted for being well administered than others.

> —**John Adams,** *Thoughts on Government,*
> PHILADELPHIA, 1776

WE OUGHT TO CONSIDER WHAT IS THE END OF government, before we determine which is the best form. Upon this point all speculative politicians will agree, that the happiness of society is the end of government, as all divines and moral philosophers will agree that the happiness of the individual is the end of man. From this principle it will follow, that the form of government which communicates ease, comfort, security, or, in one word, happiness, to the greatest number of persons, and in the greatest degree, is the best.

All sober inquirers after truth, ancient and modern, pagan and Christian, have declared that the happiness of man, as well as his dignity, consists in virtue. Confucius, Zoroaster, Socrates, Mahomet, not to mention authorities really sacred, have agreed in this.

If there is a form of government, then, whose principle and foundation is virtue, will not every sober man acknowledge it better calculated to promote the general happiness than any other form?

—**John Adams,** *Thoughts on Government,*
PHILADELPHIA, 1776

THE FOUNDATION OF EVERY GOVERNMENT IS some principle or passion in the minds of the people. The noblest principles and most generous affections in our nature, then, have the fairest chance to support the noblest and most generous models of government.

—**John Adams,** *Thoughts on Government,*
PHILADELPHIA, 1776

[T]HERE IS NO GOOD GOVERNMENT BUT WHAT
is republican. [T]he only valuable part of the
British constitution is so; because the very definition of a republic is "an empire of laws, and not
of men." [A]s a republic is the best of governments, so that particular arrangement of the powers of society, or, in other words, that form of
government which is best contrived to secure an
impartial and exact execution of the laws, is the
best of republics.

> —**John Adams,** *Thoughts on Government,*
> PHILADELPHIA, 1776

OF REPUBLICS THERE IS AN INEXHAUSTIBLE
variety, because the possible combinations of
the powers of society are capable of innumerable
variations.

> —**John Adams,** *Thoughts on Government,*
> PHILADELPHIA, 1776

AS GOOD GOVERNMENT IS AN EMPIRE OF LAWS, how shall your laws be made? In a large society, inhabiting an extensive country, it is impossible that the whole should assemble to make laws. The first necessary step, then, is to depute power from the many to a few of the most wise and good. But by what rules shall you choose your representatives? Agree upon the number and qualifications of persons who shall have the benefit of choosing, or annex this privilege to the inhabitants of a certain extent of ground.

The principal difficulty lies, and the greatest care should be employed, in constituting this representative assembly. It should be in miniature an exact portrait of the people at large. It should think, feel, reason, and act like them. That it may be the interest of this assembly to do strict justice at all times, it should be an equal representation, or, in other words, equal interests among the people should have equal interests in it. Great care should be taken to effect this, and to prevent unfair, partial, and corrupt elections.

—**John Adams,** *Thoughts on Government,*
PHILADELPHIA, 1776

[A] PEOPLE CANNOT BE LONG FREE, NOR EVER happy, whose government is in one assembly.

—John Adams, *Thoughts on Government,*
PHILADELPHIA, 1776

A CONSTITUTION FOUNDED ON THESE PRINCIPLES introduces know ledge among the people, and inspires them with a conscious dignity becoming freemen; a general emulation takes place, which causes good humor, sociability, good manners, and good morals to be general. That elevation of sentiment inspired by such a government, makes the common people brave and enterprising. That ambition which is inspired by it makes them sober, industrious, and frugal. You will find among them some elegance, perhaps, but more solidity; a little pleasure, but a great deal of business; some politeness, but more civility. If you compare such a country with the regions of domination, whether monarchical or aristocratical, you will fancy yourself in Arcadia or Elysium.

—John Adams, *Thoughts on Government,*
PHILADELPHIA, 1776

YOU AND I, MY DEAR FRIEND, HAVE BEEN SENT into life at a time when the greatest lawgivers of antiquity would have wished to live. How few of the human race have ever enjoyed an opportunity of making an election of government, more than of air, soil, or climate, for themselves or their children! When, before the present epocha, had three millions of people full power and a fair opportunity to form and establish the wisest and happiest government that human wisdom can contrive? I hope you will avail yourself and your country of that extensive learning and indefatigable industry which you possess, to assist her in the formation of the happiest governments and the best character of a great people.

   —John Adams, *Thoughts on Government,*
   PHILADELPHIA, 1776

UPON READING *[THOUGHTS ON GOVERNMENT]* I some how or other felt an uncommon affection for it; I could not help thinking it was a near relation of a very intimate Friend of mine. If I am mistaken in its descent, I know it has a near affinity to the Sentiments of that person, and tho I cannot pretend to be an adept in the art of Government, yet it looks rational that a Government of Good Laws well administered should carry with them the fairest prospect of happiness to a community, as well as to individuals.

> —**Abigail Adams** to John Adams,
> 9 MAY 1776

MAY THE FOUNDATION OF OUR NEW CONSTITUtion, be justice, Truth and Righteousness. Like the wise Mans house may it be founded upon those Rocks and then neither storms nor temptests will overthrow it.

> —**Abigail Adams** to John Adams,
> 13–14 JULY 1776

THE END OF THE INSTITUTION, MAINTENANCE, and administration of government is to secure the existence of the body politic; to protect it, and to furnish the individuals who compose it with the power of enjoying, in safety and tranquility, their natural rights and the blessings of life; and whenever these great objects are not obtained, the people have a right to alter the government, and to take measures necessary for their safety, happiness, and prosperity.

The body politic is formed by a voluntary association of individuals. It is a social compact, by which the whole people covenants with each citizen, and each citizen with the whole people, that all shall be governed by certain laws for the common good. It is the duty of the people, therefore, in framing a Constitution of Government, to provide for an equitable mode of making laws, as well as for an impartial interpretation, and a faithful execution of them; that every man may, at all times, find his security in them.

> —**John Adams,** "Report of a Constitution, or Form of Government, for the Commonwealth of Massachusetts — Preamble," 1780

I HOPE YOU WILL BE SO GOOD AS TO INFORM me of what passes, particularly what progress the

[Massachusetts] Convention makes in the
Constitution. I assure you it is more comfortable
making Constitutions in the dead of Winter at
Cambridge or Boston, than Sailing in a leaky
Ship, or climbing on foot or upon Mules over the
Mountains of Gallicia and the Pyrenees.

>—**John Adams** to Samuel Adams,
>   23 FEBRUARY 1780

THE UNITED STATES OF AMERICA HAVE EXHIBITED,
perhaps, the first example of governments erected
on the simple principles of nature; and if men are
now sufficiently enlightened to disabuse themselves of artifice, imposture, hypocrisy, and superstition, they will consider this event as an era in
their history.

>—**John Adams,** *A Defence of the*
>   *Constitutions of Government of the United*
>   *States . . . ,* 1787–1788

IT WILL NEVER BE PRETENDED THAT ANY PERSONS
employed in [forming American governments]

had interviews with the gods, or were in any degree under the inspiration of Heaven, more than those at work upon ships or houses, or laboring in merchandise or agriculture; it will forever be acknowledged that these governments were contrived merely by the use of reason and the senses. . . . Neither the people, nor their conventions, committees, nor sub-committees, considered legislation in any other light than as ordinary arts and sciences, only more important. Called without expectation, and compelled without previous inclination, though undoubtedly at the best period of time, both for England and America, suddenly to erect new systems of laws for their future government, they adopted the method of a wise architect, in erecting a new palace for the residence of his sovereign.

—**John Adams,** *A Defence of the Constitutions of Government of the United States . . . ,* 1787–1788

THIRTEEN GOVERNMENTS THUS FOUNDED ON the natural authority of the people alone, without a pretence of miracle or mystery, and which are destined to spread over the northern part of that whole quarter of the globe, are a great point gained in favor of the rights of man. The experiment is made, and has completely succeeded; it can no longer be called in question, whether authority in magistrates and obedience of citizens can be grounded on reason, morality, and the Christian religion, without the monkery of priests, or the knavery of politicians.

—John Adams, *A Defence of the Constitutions of Government of the United States . . . ,* 1787–1788

THE SYSTEMS OF LEGISLATORS ARE EXPERIMENTS made on human life and manners, society and government. [Lawgivers] may be compared to philosophers making experiments on the elements. Unhappily, political experiments cannot be made in a laboratory, nor determined in a few hours. The operation once begun, runs over whole quarters of the globe, and is not finished in many thousands of years.

—John Adams, *A Defence of the Constitutions of Government of the United States . . . ,* 1787–1788

THE INSTITUTIONS NOW MADE IN AMERICA WILL not wholly wear out for thousands of years. It is of the last importance, then, that they should begin right. If they set out wrong, they will never be able to return, unless it be by accident, to the right path.

> —**John Adams,** *A Defence of the Constitutions of Government of the United States . . . ,* 1787–1788

IN EVERY REPUBLIC, —— IN THE SMALLEST AND most popular, in the larger and more aristocratical, as well as in the largest and most monarchical, —— we have observed a multitude of curious and ingenious inventions to balance, in their turn, all those powers, to check the passions peculiar to them, and to control them from rushing into those exorbitancies to which they are most addicted.

> —**John Adams,** *A Defence of the Constitutions of Government of the United States . . . ,* 1787–1788

[L]ET US COMPARE EVERY CONSTITUTION WE have seen with those of the United States of America, and we shall have no reason to blush for our country. On the contrary, we shall feel the strongest motives to fall upon our knees, in gratitude to heaven for having been graciously pleased to give us birth and education in that country, and for having destined us to live under her laws! . . . Our people are undoubtedly sovereign; all the landed and other property is in the hands of the citizens; not only of their representatives, but their senators and governors, are annually chosen; there are no hereditary titles, honors, offices, or distinctions; the legislative, executive, and judicial powers are carefully separated from each other; the powers of the one, the few, and the many are nicely balanced in the legislatures; trials by jury are preserved in all their glory, and there is no standing army; the *habeas corpus* is in full force; the press is the most free in the world. Where all these circumstances take place, it is unnecessary to add that the laws alone can govern.

—**John Adams,** *A Defence of the Constitutions of Government of the United States . . . ,* 1787–1788

IT IS THE MASTER ARTIST ALONE WHO FINISHES his building, his picture, or his clock. The present actors on the stage have been too little prepared by their early views, and too much occupied with turbulent scenes, to do more than they have done. Impartial justice will confess that it is astonishing they have been able to do so much. It is for the young to make themselves masters of what their predecessors have been able to comprehend and accomplish but imperfectly.

—John Adams, *A Defence of the Constitutions of Government of the United States . . . ,* 1787–1788

THE MAGNITUDE OF TERRITORY, THE POPULATION, the wealth and commerce, and especially the rapid growth of the United States, have shown such a government [the Articles of Confederation] to be inadequate to their wants; and the new system [the Constitution of the United States], which seems admirably calculated to unite their interests and affections, and bring them to an uniformity of principles and sentiments, is equally well combined to unite their wills and forces as a single nation. A result of accommodation cannot be supposed to reach the ideas of perfection of any one; but the conception of such an idea, and the deliberate union of so great and various a people in such a plan, is, without all partiality or prejudice, if not the greatest exertion of human understanding, the greatest single effort of national deliberation that the world has ever seen. That it may be improved is not to be doubted, and provision is made for that purpose in the report itself. A people who could conceive, and can adopt it, we need not fear will be able to amend it, when, by experience, its inconveniences and imperfections shall be seen and felt.

> —John Adams, *A Defence of the Constitutions of Government of the United States . . . ,* 1787–1788

THE DIFFICULTY OF BRINGING MILLIONS TO agree in any measure, to act by any rule, can never be conceived by him who has not tried it.

> —John Adams to Richard Price, 19 APRIL 1790

THE SOCIAL COMPACT AND THE LAWS MUST
be reduced to Writing. Obedience to them becomes a national Habit and they cannot be
changed but by Revolutions which are costly
things. Men will be too Œconomical of their
Blood and Property to have recourse to them
very frequently.

> —**John Adams** to Thomas Jefferson,
> 11 MAY 1794

THE CONSTITUTION, IT IS TRUE, MUST SPEAK FOR
itself, and be interpreted by its own phraseology;
yet the history and state of things at the time may
be consulted to elucidate the meaning of words,
and determine the bonâ fide intention of the
Convention.

> —**John Adams** to Josiah Quincy,
> 9 FEBRUARY 1811

POWER MUST BE OPPOSED TO POWER, FORCE TO force, strength to strength, interest to interest, as well as reason to reason, eloquence to eloquence, and passion to passion. . . .

A CONSTITUTION IS A STANDARD, A PILLAR, AND a bond when it is understood, approved and beloved. But without this intelligence and attachment, it might as well be a kite or balloon, flying in the air. . . .

THESE MACHINES CALLED CONSTITUTIONS ARE not to be taken to pieces and cleaned or mended so easily as a watch.

> —**John Adams,** marginal notes (1812) on
> Mary Wollstonecraft, *Historical and Moral
> View of the Origin and Progress of the French
> Revolution,* 1794

THE ART OF LAWGIVING IS NOT SO EASY AS THAT of Architecture or Painting. . . . I may refine too much. I may be an Enthusiast. But I think a free Government is necessarily a complicated Piece of Machinery, the nice and exact Adjustment of whose Springs Wheels and Weights are not yet well comprehended by the Artists of the Age and still less by the People.

—**John Adams** to Thomas Jefferson,
19 MAY 1821

Education

LAWS FOR THE LIBERAL EDUCATION OF YOUTH,
especially of the lower class of people, are so extremely wise and useful, that, to a humane and
generous mind, no expense for this purpose
would be thought extravagant.

> —**John Adams**, *Thoughts on Government,*
> PHILADELPHIA, 1776

IF YOU COMPLAIN OF NEGLECT OF EDUCATION
in sons, What shall I say with regard to daughters,
who every day experience the want of it. . . . I
most sincerely wish that some more liberal plan
might be laid and executed for the Benefit of the
rising Generation, and that our new constitution
may be distinguished for Learning and Virtue. If
we mean to have Heroes, Statesmen, and
Philosophers, we should have learned women.

The world perhaps would laugh at me, and accuse me of vanity. But you I know have a mind too enlarged and liberal to disregard the Sentiment. If much depends as is allowed upon the early Education of youth and the first principals which are instilld take the deepest root, great benefit must arise from litirary accomplishments in women.

> —**Abigail Adams** to John Adams,
>   14 AUGUST 1776

IMPROVE YOUR UNDERSTANDING FOR ACQUIRING useful knowledge and virtue, such as will render you an ornament to society, an Honour to your Country, and a Blessing to your parents. Great Learning and superior abilities, should you ever possess them, will be of little value and small Estimation, unless Virtue, Honour, Truth and integrety are added to them. Adhere to those religious Sentiments and principals which are easily instilled into your mind and remember that you are accountable to your Maker for all your words and actions. Let me injoin it upon you to attend constantly and steadfastly to the precepts and instructions of your Father as you value the happiness of your Mother and your own welfare. I had much rather you should have found your Grave in the ocean you have crossd or any untimely death crop you in your Infant years, rather than see you an immoral profligate or a Graceless child.

—**Abigail Adams** to John Quincy Adams, 10[?] JUNE 1778

THESE ARE TIMES IN WHICH A GENIOUS WOULD wish to live. It is not in the still calm of life, or in the repose of a pacific station, that great characters are formed. . . . The Habits of a vigorous mind are formed in contending with difficulties. All History will convince you of this, and that wisdom and penetration are the fruits of experience, not the Lessons of retirement and leisure. Great necessities call out great virtues. When a mind is raised, and animated by scenes that engage the Heart, then those qualities which would otherways lay dormant, wake into Life, and form the Character of the Hero and the Statesman.

—**Abigail Adams** to John Quincy Adams, 19 JANUARY 1780

YOU MUST NOT BE A SUPERFICIAL OBSERVER,
but study Men and Manners that you may be
Skilfull in both. Tis said of Socrates, that the oracle
pronounced him the wisest of all Men living because he judiciously made choice of Humane
Nature for the object of his Thoughts. Youth is
the proper season for observation and attention —
a mind unincumbered with cares may seek instruction and draw improvement from all the
objects which surround it. The earlier in life you
accustome yourself to consider objects with attention, the easier will your progress be, and more
sure and successful your enterprizes. What a
harvest of true knowledge and learning may you
gather from the numberless varied Scenes through
which you pass if you are not wanting in your
own assiduity and endeavours. Let your ambition
be engaged to become eminent, but above all
things support a virtuous character, and remember
that "an Honest Man is the Noblest work of God."

　　　　—**Abigail Adams** to John Quincy Adams,
　　　21 JANUARY 1781

AMIDST YOUR ARDOUR FOR GREEK AND LATIN
I hope you will not forget your mother Tongue.
Read Somewhat in the English Poets every day.
You will find them elegant, entertaining and in-
structive Companions, through your whole Life.
In all the Disquisitions you have heard concerning
the Happiness of Life, has it ever been recom-
mended to you to read Poetry? To one who has a
Taste, the Poets serve to fill up Time which
would otherwise pass in Idleness, Languor, or
Vice. You will never be alone, with a Poet in
your Poket. You will never have an idle Hour.

> —**John Adams** to John Quincy Adams,
> 14 MAY 1781

HAVE YOU KEPT A REGULAR JOURNAL? IF YOU
have not, you will be likely to forget most of
the Observations you have made. If you have
omitted this Usefull Exercise, let me advise you
to recommence it, immediately. Let it be your
Amusement, to minute every day, whatever you
may have seen or heard worth Notice. One con-
tracts a Fondness for Writing by Use. We learn to
write readily, and what is of more importance,

We think, and improve our Judgments, by com-
mitting our Thoughts to Paper.

>   —**John Adams** to John Quincy Adams,
>   14 MAY 1783

YOU WILL FIND YOURSELVES ON YOUR ARRIVAL
at Liverpool in a new World. Every thing will
surprise you. Be upon your guard. Remember
your youth and inexperience, your total
Ignorance of the great World, be always modest,
ingenuous, teachable, never assuming or forward,
treat all People with respect; preserve the
Character of youthful Americans, let nothing un-
becoming ever escape your lips or your
Behaviour. You have Characters to Support,
Reputations to acquire; I may Say, you have the
Character of your Country, at least of its
Chil[d]hood and youth to Support.

>   —**John Adams** to his grandsons, George
>   Washington Adams and John Adams 2d,
>   3 MAY 1815

I WISH YOU TO HAVE EACH A PENCIL BOOK,
always in your Pockett, by which you may
minute on the Spot any remarkable thing you
may See or hear. A pocket Ink horn, any cheap
thing of the kind, and a Sheet or two of paper,
ought always to be about you. A Journal; a Diary
is indispensible. . . . Without a minute Diary, your
Travels, will be no better than the flight of Birds,
through the Air. They will leave no trace behind
them. Whatever you write preserve. I have
burned, Bushells of my Silly notes, in fitts of
Impatience and humiliation, which I would now
give anything to recover.

> —**John Adams** to his grandsons, George
> Washington Adams and John Adams 2d,
> 3 MAY 1815

French Revolution

I CONSIDER ALL REASONING UPON FRENCH
Affairs of little moment. The Fates must determine hereafter as they have done heretofore.
Reasoning has been all lost. Passion, Prejudice,
Interest, Necessity has governed and will govern;
and a Century must roll away before any perma-
nent and quiet System will be established. An
Amelioration of human affairs I hope and believe
will be the result, but You and I must look down
from the Battlements of Heaven if We ever have
the Pleasure of Seeing it.

>   —**John Adams** to Thomas Jefferson,
>   31 JANUARY 1796

THE FIRST TIME, THAT YOU AND I DIFFERED IN
opinion on any material Question was after your
Arrival from Europe; and that point was the

French Revolution. You was well persuaded in your own mind that the Nation would succeed in establishing a free Republican Government: I was as well persuaded, in mine, that a project of such a Government, over five and twenty millions people, when four and twenty millions and five hundred thousands of them could neither write nor read: was as unnatural irrational and impracticable; as it would be over the Elephants Lions Tigers Panthers Wolves and Bears in the Royal Menagerie, at Versailles.

—**John Adams** to Thomas Jefferson,
   13 JULY 1813

History and Memory

IT WAS THIS GREAT STRUGGLE THAT POPULATED America. It was not religion alone, as is commonly supposed; but it was a love of universal liberty, and a hatred, a dread, a horror, of the infernal confederacy [of the canon law and the feudal law], . . . that projected, conducted, and accomplished the settlement of America.

> **—John Adams,** "A Dissertation on the Canon and Feudal Law," 1765

THE HISTORY OF GREECE SHOULD BE TO OUR countrymen what is called in many families on the continent a *boudoir*, an octagonal apartment in a house, with a full-length mirror on every side, and another in the ceiling. The use of it is, when any of the young ladies, or young gentlemen if you will, are at any time a little out of humor, they may retire to a place where, in whatever direction they turn their eyes, they see their own faces and figures multiplied without end. By thus beholding their own beautiful persons, and seeing, at the same time, the deformity brought upon them by their anger, they may recover their tempers and their charms together.

> —**John Adams,** *A Defence of the Constitutions of Government of the United States . . . , 1787–1788*

A SCIENCE CERTAINLY COMPREHENDS ALL THE principles in nature which belong to the subject. The principles in nature which relate to government cannot all be known, without a knowledge of the history of mankind.

> —**John Adams,** *A Defence of the Constitutions of Government of the United States . . . , 1787–1788*

THE HISTORY OF OUR REVOLUTION WILL BE ONE continued lie from one end to the other. The essence of the whole will be that Dr. Franklin's electrical rod smote the earth and out sprang General Washington. That Franklin electrified him with his rod — and thenceforward these two conducted all the policies, negotiations, legislatures and war.

> —**John Adams** to Benjamin Rush,
>   4 APRIL 1790

THE DESTRUCTION OF ANCIENT BOOKS HAS NOT been accidental. The lost classics, the lost infidels, and the lost heretics were probably all destroyed by design, either of civil despots or ecclesiastical craft and fraud.

> —**John Adams,** marginal note on
>   Joseph Priestley, *Early Opinions*
>   *Concerning Jesus Christ*

I AM HALF INCLINED TO BE VERY ANGRY WITH you for destroying the anecdotes and documents you had collected for private memoirs of the American Revolution. From the memoirs of individuals the true springs of events and the real motives of actions are to be made known to posterity.

—**John Adams** to Benjamin Rush,
4 DECEMBER 1805

I HAVE SOMETIMES THOUGHT THAT THE PUBLIC opinion is never right concerning present measures or future events. The secret of affairs is never known to the public till after the event, and often not then. Even in the freest and most popular governments, events are preparing by causes that are at work in secret, known only to a very few, partially communicated in confidence to a few others, but never fully made known to the people till long after all is past. And very often the real springs, motives, and causes remain secret in the breasts of a few, and perhaps of one, and perish with their keepers. . . .

—**John Adams** to Benjamin Rush,
23 JULY 1806

IF WE WERE TO COUNT OUR YEARS BY THE
revolutions we have witnessed, we might number
them with the antidiluvians. So rapid have been
the changes, that the mind, though fleet in its
progress, has been outstripped by them; and we
are left like statues, gazing at what we can neither
fathom nor comprehend.

> —**Abigail Adams** to Mercy Otis Warren,
> 1807

I DOUBT WHETHER FAITHFUL HISTORY EVER WAS
or ever can be written. 300 years after the event it
cannot be written without offending some powerful and popular individual family party, some
statesman, some general, some prince, some priest
or some philosopher. The world will go on always ignorant of itself, its past history, and future
destiny.

> —**John Adams** to Benjamin Rush,
> 31 AUGUST 1809

CAN YOU ACCOUNT FOR THE APATHY, THE
antipathy of this nation to their own history? Is
there not a repugnance to the thought of looking
back? While thousands of frivolous novels are
read with eagerness and got by heart, the history
of our own native country is not only neglected
but despised and abhorred.

     —**John Adams** to Thomas McKean,
       31 AUGUST 1813

Human Nature

A PEN IS CERTAINLY AN EXCELLENT INSTRUMENT, to fix a Mans Attention and to inflame his Ambition.

> —**John Adams,** diary entry,
> 14 NOVEMBER 1760

THERE IS NOTHING IN THE SCIENCE OF HUMAN nature more curious, or that deserves a critical attention from every order of men so much, as that principle which moral writers have distinguished by the name of self-deceit. This principle is the spurious offspring of self-love; and is, perhaps, the source of far the greatest and worst part of the vices and calamities among mankind.

> —**John Adams,** "On Self-Delusion,"
> *Boston Gazette,* No. 439,
> 29 AUGUST 1763

. . . [I]T HAPPENS THAT NO IMPROVEMENTS IN
science or literature, no reformation in religion or
morals, nor any rectification of mistaken measures
in government, can be made without opposition
from numbers, who, flattering themselves that
their own intentions are pure, (how sinister soever
they may be in fact) will reproach impure designs
to others, or, fearing a detriment to their interest
or a mortification to their passions from the inno-
vation, will even think it lawful directly and
knowingly to falsify the motives and characters of
the innocent.

> —**John Adams,** "On Self-Delusion,"
> *Boston Gazette,* No. 439,
> 29 AUGUST 1763

LET NOT WRITERS NOR STATESMEN DECEIVE
themselves. The springs of their own conduct and
opinions are not always so clear and pure, nor are
those of their antagonists in politics always so pol-
luted and corrupted, as they believe, and would
have the world believe too. Many readers and
private persons can see virtues and talents on each

side; and to their sorrow they have not yet seen any side altogether free from atrocious vices, extreme ignorance, and most lamentable folly.

> —**John Adams,** "On Self-Delusion,"
> *Boston Gazette,* No. 439,
> 29 AUGUST 1763

HUMAN NATURE ITSELF IS EVERMORE AN advocate for liberty. There is also in human nature a resentment of injury and indignation against wrong; a love of truth, and a veneration for virtue. . . . If the people are capable of understanding, seeing, and feeling the difference between true and false, right and wrong, virtue and vice, to what better principle can the friends of mankind apply, than to the sense of this difference?

> —**John Adams,** *Novanglus,*
> 1774–1775

THE HUMAN MIND IS NOT NATURALLY THE clearest atmosphere; but the clouds and vapors

which have been raised in it by the artifices of
temporal and spiritual tyrants, have made it impossible to see objects in it distinctly.

    —**John Adams,** *Novanglus*
     (1774–1775)

THE INSTRUCTIONS OF MY OWN GRANDMAMMA
are as fresh upon my mind this day as any I ever
received from my own parents and made as lasting and powerful impressions. Every virtuous example has powerfull impressions in early youth.
Many years of vice and vicious examples do not
erase from the mind seeds sown in early life.
They take a deep root, and tho often crop'd
will spring again.

    —**Abigail Adams** to John Adams,
     9 OCTOBER 1775

I AM MORE AND MORE CONVINCED THAT MAN
is a dangerous creature; and that power whether
vested in many or a few is ever grasping, and,
like the grave, cries give, give. The great fish

swallow up the small, and he who is most strenuous for the Rights of the people, when vested with power, is as eager after the prerogatives of Government. You tell me of degrees of perfection to which Humane Nature is capable of arriving, and I believe it, but at the same time lament that our admiration should arise from the scarcity of the instances.

> **—Abigail Adams** to John Adams,
> 27 NOVEMBER 1775

WE OUGHT NEVER TO DESPAIR OF *WHAT HAS been once accomplished*. How many things have the Idea of impossible been annexed to, that have become easy to those who knew how to take advantage of Time, opportunity, lucky Moments, the Faults of others, different dispositions and an infinite Number of other circumstances.

> **—Abigail Adams** to John Adams,
> 27 MAY 1776

I BELIEVE THERE IS NO ONE PRINCIPLE, WHICH
predominates in human Nature so much in every
stage of Life, from the Cradle to the Grave in
Males and females, old and young, black and
white, rich and poor, high and low, as this Passion
for Superiority. . . . Every human Being compares
itself in its own Imagination, with every other
round about it, and will find some Superiority
over every other real or imaginary, or it will die
of Grief and Vexation.

> —John Adams to Abigail Adams,
>   22 MAY 1777

. . . I HAVE WELL FIXED IT IN MY MIND AS A
Principle, that every Nation has a Right to that
Religion and Government, which it chooses, and
as long as any People please themselves in these
great Points, I am determined they shall not dis-
please me.

> —John Adams to Abigail Adams,
>   3 JUNE 1778

MY DEAR COUNTRY MEN! HOW SHALL I
perswade you, to avoid the Plague of Europe?
Luxury has as many and as bewitching Charms,
on your Side of the Ocean as on this — and
Luxury, wherever she goes, effaces from human
Nature the Image of the Divinity. If I had power
I would forever banish and exclude from
America, all Gold, Silver, Precious Stones,
Alabaster, Marble, Silk, Velvet and Lace.

> —**John Adams** to Abigail Adams,
> 3 JUNE 1778

IT IS FROM A WIDE AND EXTENSIVE VIEW OF
mankind that a just and true estimate can be
formed of the powers of human nature.

> —**Abigail Adams** to John Quincy Adams,
> 26 MAY 1781

I CANNOT HELP ADDING AN OBSERVATION WHICH
appears pertinant to me: that there is an ingredi-
ent necessary in a Mans composition towards happiness, which people of feeling would do well to

acquire — a certain respect for the follies of Mankind. For there are so many fools whom the opinion of the world entitles to regard, whom accident has placed in heights of which they are unworthy, that he who cannot restrain his contempt or indignation at the sight, will be too often Quarreling with the disposal of things to realish that share, which is allotted to himself.

> —**Abigail Adams** to John Adams,
> 15 DECEMBER 1783

. . . [L]ET NO PERSON SAY WHAT THEY WOULD or would not do, since we are not judges for ourselves till circumstances call us to act.

> —**Abigail Adams** to John Adams,
> 25 MAY 1784

[T]HERE CAN BE NO EMPLOYMENT MORE disagreable than that of weighing Merit, by the Grain and Scruple, because the world very seldom form an opinion of a Man precisely the same with his own, and therefore the Scales will always be objected to, as not justly ballanced. It is worse than the Business of a Portrait Painter, as Men are generally better Satisfied with their own Talents and Virtues, than even with their Faces.

—**John Adams** to Thomas Jefferson,
13 DECEMBER 1785

WHAT IS THE CHIEF END OF MAN? IS A SUBJECT well worth the investigation of every rational being. What, indeed, is life, or its enjoyments, without settled principle, laudable purposes, mental exertions, and internal comfort, that sunshine of the soul, and how are these to be acquired in a hurry and tumult of the world?

—**Abigail Adams** to Mary Cranch,
20 JANUARY 1787

LESSONS MY DEAR SIR, ARE NEVER WANTING. Life and History are full. The Loss of Paradise, by eating a forbidden apple, has been many Thousand years a Lesson to Mankind; but not much regarded. Moral Reflections, wise Maxims, religious Terrors, have little Effect upon Nations when they contradict a present Passion, Prejudice, Imagination, Enthusiasm or Caprice. . . . I have long been settled in my own opinion, that neither Philosophy, nor Religion, nor Morality, nor Wisdom, nor Interest, will ever govern nations or Parties, against their Vanity, their Pride, their Resentment or Revenge, or their Avarice or Ambition. Nothing but Force and Power and Strength can restrain them.

—**John Adams** to Thomas Jefferson,
9 OCTOBER 1787

HUMAN NATURE IS AS INCAPABLE NOW OF going through revolutions with temper and sobriety, with patience and prudence, or without fury and madness, as it was among the Greeks so long ago.

—**John Adams,** *A Defence of the Constitutions of Government of the United States . . . ,* 1787–1788

WE CANNOT PRESUME THAT A MAN IS GOOD OR bad, merely because his father was one or the other; and we should always inform ourselves first, whether the virtues or talents are inherited, before we yield our confidence. Wise men beget fools, and honest men knaves. . . .

> —John Adams, *A Defence of the Constitutions of Government of the United States . . . ,* 1787–1788

THERE IS IN EVERY NATION AND PEOPLE UNDER heaven a large proportion of persons who take no rational and prudent precautions to preserve what they have, much less to acquire more. Indolence is the natural character of man, to such a degree that nothing but the necessities of hunger, thirst, and other wants equally pressing, can stimulate him to action, until education is introduced in civilized societies, and the strongest motives of ambition to excel in arts, trades, and professions are established in the minds of all men.

> —John Adams, *A Defence of the Constitutions of Government of the United States . . . ,* 1787–1788

CAN YOU FIND A PEOPLE WHO NEVER WILL
be divided in opinion? who will always be
unanimous?

> —John Adams, *A Defence of the
> Constitutions of Government of the United
> States . . . ,* 1787–1788

THOUGH WE ALLOW BENEVOLENCE AND
generous affections to exist in the human breast,
yet every moral theorist will admit the selfish passions in the generality of man to be the strongest.

> —John Adams, *A Defence of the
> Constitutions of Government of the United
> States . . . ,* 1787–1788

NATIONAL PRIDE IS AS NATURAL AS SELF-LOVE,
or family pride, the pride of one city, county, or
province, or the esprit de corps of an army, navy,
an ecclesiastical order, a body of merchants or
tradesmen, farmers, or comedians. It is, at present,

the bulwark of defense to all nations. When it is lost, a nation sinks below the character of man.

> —**John Adams,** marginal note (1790s) on Turgot's letter to Dr. Price, 1778

I BEG LEAVE TO PROPOSE THAT THE WHOLE earth should be divided into independent re-publics of six miles square; that wars should for-ever cease, commerce be free as light and air, as well as religion; that all men should be wise and virtuous; no more jealousy, envy, avarice or ambi-tion. Amen.

> —**John Adams,** sarcastic marginal note (1790s) on Turgot's letter to Dr. Price, 1778

WHAT IS PHILOSOPHY BUT THE STUDY OF THE world and its cause? Man is a riddle to himself. The world is a riddle to him. He puzzles to find a key, and this puzzle is called philosophy.

> —**John Adams,** marginal note on Joseph Priestley, *Early Opinions Concerning Jesus Christ*

[ARE] THE FINE AND DELICATE SENSIBILITIES OF
the soul . . . a real blessing[?] They so often are
wounded by the insensible by the unfeeling beings
which surround them of which much the larger
portion of mankind are composed. . . . [L]ike the
rose of Cowper they are shaken by the rude blast
— or witherd by cold neglect, instead of having
the fear of sorrow wiped away by the sympathiz-
ing hand of congenial tenderness. Yet who that
possesses them would be willing to exchange
them for a cold hearted apathy, and a stoical indif-
ference. A fine tuned instrument is soonest put
out of order, yet what lover of musick would wish
to possess in preference an ordinary instrument?

    —Abigail Adams to Ann Harrod,
      19 FEBRUARY 1805

BY PRUDENCE I MEAN THAT DELIBERATION AND
caution which aims at no ends but good ones, and
good ones by none but fair means, and then carefully adjusts and proportions its good means to its
good ends. Without this virtue there can be no
other. Justice itself cannot exist without it. A

disposition to render to everyone his right is of no use without prudence to judge of what is his right and skill to perform it.

> —**John Adams** to Benjamin Rush,
> 1 SEPTEMBER 1807

I AM WEARY OF CONTEMPLATING NATIONS FROM the lowest and most beastly degradations of human Life, to the highest Refinement of Civilization. I am weary of Philosophers, Theologians, Politicians, and Historians. They are immense Masses of Absurdities, Vices and Lies. Montesquieu had sense enough to say in Jest, that all our Knowledge might be comprehended in twelve Pages in Duodecimo; and, I believe him, in earnest. I could express my Faith in shorter terms. He who loves the Workman and his Work, and does what he can to preserve and improve it, shall be accepted of him.

> —**John Adams** to Thomas Jefferson,
> 28 JUNE 1812

I HAVE NO IDOLATRY FOR POLITICIANS OR
warriors. Who would not prefer Hippocrates to
Alexander or Demosthenes? Every discovery, invention, or improvement in science, especially
medical science, is lasting. Political and military
glories transient as the wind. Solon and Lycurgus
have passed away, and what good have they done?
It would be republican blasphemy to say that
Pisastrus, the tyrant, did more good than both.
Yet history would countenance a doubt.

> —John Adams to Benjamin Rush,
> 22 FEBRUARY 1813

THERE ARE CRITICAL MOMENTS, WHEN FACTION,
whether in Church or State, will stick at nothing.
Confidence of Friendship the most sacred, is
but a cobweb tie. How few! Oh how few are
the exceptions! I could name many Cases of the
rule. . . .

> —John Adams to Thomas Jefferson,
> 25 JUNE 1813

CHECKS AND BALLANCES, JEFFERSON, HOWEVER you and your Party may have ridiculed them, are our only Security, for the progress of Mind, as well as the Security of Body. Every Species of these Christians would persecute Deists, as soon as either Sect would persecute another, if it had unchecked and unballanced Power. Nay, the Deists would persecute Christians, and Atheists would persecute Deists, with as unrelenting Cruelty, as any Christians would persecute them or one another. Know thyself, Human Nature!

    —**John Adams** to Thomas Jefferson,
      25 JUNE 1813

THIS WORLD IS A MIXTURE OF THE SUBLIME AND the beautiful, the base and contemptible, the whimsical and ridiculous, (According to our narrow Sense, and triffling Feelings). It is a Riddle and an Enigma. You need not be surprised then, if I should descend from these Heights to an egregious Trifle.

    —**John Adams** to Thomas Jefferson,
      15 SEPTEMBER 1813

THAT ALL MEN ARE BORN TO EQUAL RIGHTS IS true. Every being has a right to his own, as clear, as moral, as sacred, as any other being has. This is as indubitable as a moral government in the universe. But to teach that all men are born with equal powers and faculties, to equal influence in society, to equal property and advantages through life, is as gross a fraud, as glaring an imposition on the credulity of the people, as ever was practised by monks, by Druids, by Brahmins, by priests of the immortal Lama, or by the self-styled philosophers of the French revolution.

—**John Adams** to John Taylor,
19 APRIL 1814

[A]CCORDING TO THE FEW LIGHTS THAT REMAIN to Us, We may say that the Eighteenth Century, notwithstanding all its Errors and Vices has been, of all that are past, the most honourable to human Nature. Knowledge and Virtue were increased and diffused, Arts, Sciences useful to Men, ameliorating their condition, were improved, more than in any former equal Period.

—**John Adams** to Thomas Jefferson,
13 NOVEMBER 1815

GRIEF DRIVES MEN INTO HABITS OF SERIOUS
Reflection sharpens the Understanding and soft-
ens the heart; it compells them to arrouse their
Reason, to asserts its Empire over their Passions
Propensities and Prejudices; to elevate them to a
Superiority over all human Events; to give them
[the imperturbable tranquility of a happy heart];
in short to make them Stoicks and Christians.

    —**John Adams** to Thomas Jefferson,
    6 MAY 1816

AFTER ALL, AS GRIEF IS A PAIN, IT STANDS IN THE
Predicament of all other Evil and the great question Occurs what is the Origin and what the final
cause of Evil. This perhaps is known only to
Omnicience. We poor Mortals have nothing to
do with it, but to fabricate all the good We can
out of all inevitable Evils, and to avoid all that are
avoidable, and many such there are, among which
are our own unnecessary Apprehensions and
imaginary Fears. Though Stoical Apathy is impossible, Yet Patience and Resignation and tranquility

may be acquired by Consideration in a great degree, very much for the hapiness of life.

 —**John Adams** to Thomas Jefferson,
   6 MAY 1816

I ALMOST SHUDDER AT THE THOUGHT OF
alluding to the most fatal Example of the Abuses
of Grief, which the History of Man kind has preserved. The Cross. Consider what Calamities that
Engine of Grief has produced! With the rational
Respect that is due to it, knavish Priests have
added Prostitutions of it, that fill or might fill the
blackest and bloodiest pages of human History.

 —**John Adams** to Thomas Jefferson,
   3 SEPTEMBER 1816

THE VAST PROSPECT OF MANKIND, WHICH THESE
Books have passed in Review before me, from
the most ancient records, histories, traditions and
Fables that remain to Us, to the present day, has
sickened my very Soul, and almost reconciled me

to Swifts Travels among The Yahoo's. Yet I never can be a Misanthrope. Homo Sum ["I am a man"]. I must hate myself before I can hate my Fellow Men: and that I cannot and will not do. No! I will not hate any of them, base, brutal and devilish as some of them have been to me.

> —**John Adams** to Thomas Jefferson,
> 19 APRIL 1817

I ANSWER YOUR QUESTION, IS DEATH AN EVIL? It is not an Evil. It is a blessing to the individual, and to the world. Yet we ought not to wish for it till life becomes insupportable; we must wait the pleasure and convenience of this great teacher.

> —**John Adams** to Thomas Jefferson,
> 11 JUNE 1822

I HOPE ONE DAY YOUR LETTERS WILL BE ALL published in volumes; they will not always appear Orthodox, or liberal in politicks; but they will exhibit a Mass of Taste, Sense, Literature and Science, presented in a sweet simplicity and a neat

elegance of Stile, which will be read with delight
in future ages. . . . Your stationary bill alone for
paper, Quills, Ink, Wafers, Wax, Sand and
Pounce, must have amounted to enough to maintain a small family.

> —**John Adams** to Thomas Jefferson,
>   12 JULY 1822

IT IS MELANCHOLY TO CONTEMPLATE THE CRUEL
wars, dissolutions of Countries, and ocians of
blood which must occure, before rational principles, and rational systems of Government can pre-
vail and be established. But as these are inevitable
we must content ourselves with the consolations
which you from sound and sure reasons so clearly
suggest.

> —**John Adams** to Thomas Jefferson,
>   18 SEPTEMBER 1823

John Adams and Abigail Adams on Themselves

I AM BUT AN ORDINARY MAN. THE TIMES
alone have destined me to Fame — and even
these have not been able to give me, much. . . .
Yet some great Events, some cutting Expressions,
some mean Scandals, Hypocrisies, have at Times,
thrown this Assemblage of Sloth, Sleep, and little-
ness into Rage a little like a Lion.

> —**John Adams,** diary entry,
> 26 APRIL 1779

I KNOW NOT THE REASON BUT THERE IS SOME
Strange Attraction between the North Parish in
Braintree and my Heart. It is a remarkable Spot.
It has vomited Forth more Fire than Mount Etna.
It has produced three mortals, Hancock and two
Adams's, who have, with the best Intentions in
the World, set the World in a blaze. I say two
Adams's because the Head of the Senate [Samuel
Adams] sprung from thence as his father was born
there. — Glorious however as the flame is, I wish
I could put it out. — Some People say I was born
for such Times. It is true I was born to be in such
times but was not made for them. They affect too
tenderly my Heart.

> —**John Adams** to Abigail Adams, around
>   15 AUGUST 1782

FOR A MAN WHO HAS BEEN THIRTY YEARS
rolling like a stone never three years in the same
Place, it is no very pleasant Speculation, to cross
the seas with a Family, in a State of Uncertainty
what is to be his fate; what reception he shall
meet at home; whether he shall set down in private Life to his Plough; or push into turbulent
Scenes of Sedition and Tumult; whether be sent

to Congress, or a Convention or God knows what. — If it lay in my Power, I would take a Vow, to retire to my little Turnip yard, and never again quit it. — I often feel a violent disposition to take some Resolution and swear to it. But upon the whole, it is best to preserve my Liberty to do as I please according to Circumstances.

    —**John Adams** to Thomas Jefferson,
     1 MARCH 1787

I HAVE SPENT MY SUMMER SO DELICIOUSLY IN farming that I return to the old Story of Politicks with great Reluctance. The Earth is Grateful. You find it so, I dare say. I wish We could both say the Same of its Inhabitants.

    —**John Adams** to Thomas Jefferson,
     21 NOVEMBER 1794

YOU HEAR I AM STILL FACETIOUS UPON SOME subjects. But my facetiousness, you know, was always awkward and seldom understood. When I was young, I had two intimate friends, Jonathan Sewall and Daniel Leonard — they both went away to England in 1775. They used to tell me I had a little capillary vein of satire meandering about in my soul, and it broke out so strangely, suddenly, and irregularly that it was impossible ever to foresee when it would come or how it would appear. I have thought of this sometimes and have had reasons enough to do so. . . . You will expect from me the garrulity of narrative old age, and here you have it.

> —**John Adams** to Benjamin Rush,
> 27 FEBRUARY 1805

IF MY CONDUCT CANNOT BE JUSTIFIED BY reason, justice, and the public good, without the smallest aid from the prejudices or caprices of the people, or from the judgment of any single individual on earth, I pray that it may be condemned.

> —**John Adams** to Benjamin Rush,
> 7 JULY 1805

MY TEMPER IN GENERAL HAS BEEN TRANQUIL, except when any instance of extraordinary madness, deceit, hypocrisy, ingratitude, treachery or perfidy, has suddenly struck me. Then I have always been irascible enough, and in three or four instances, very extraordinary ones, too much so. The storm, however, never lasted for half an hour, and anger never rested in the bosom.

> —John Adams to Skelton Jones,
> 11 MARCH 1809

MAUSOLEUMS, STATUES, MONUMENTS WILL NEVER be erected to me. I wish them not. Panegyrical romances will never be written, nor flattering orations spoken, to transmit me to posterity in brilliant colors. No, nor in true colors. All but the last I loathe. Yet I will not die wholly unlamented.

> —John Adams to Benjamin Rush,
> 23 MARCH 1809

I CANNOT CONTEMPLATE HUMAN AFFAIRS,
without laughing or crying. I choose to laugh.

   —**John Adams** to Thomas Jefferson,
      15 JULY 1817

FROM MY INFANCY I HAVE ALWAYS FELT A GREAT
inclination to visit the Mother Country as tis
call'd and had nature formed me of the other
Sex, I should certainly have been a rover. And
although this desire is greatly diminished owing
partly I believe to maturer years, but more to the
unnatural treatment which this our poor America
has received from her, I yet retain a curiosity to
know what ever is valuable in her.

   —**Abigail Adams** to Isaac Smith,
      20 APRIL 1771

MY PEN IS ALWAYS FREER THAN MY TONGUE. I
have wrote many things to you that I suppose I
never could have talk'd.

   —**Abigail Adams** to John Adams,
      22 OCTOBER 1775

I HAVE POSSESSION OF MY AUNTS CHAMBER IN which you know is a very convenient pretty closet with a window which looks into her flower Garden. In this closet are a number of Book Shelves, which are but poorly furnished, however I have a pretty little desk or cabinet here where I write all my Letters and keep my papers un-mollested by any one. I do not covet my Neighbours Goods, but I should like to be the owner of such conveniances. I always had a fancy for a closet with a window which I could more peculiarly call my own. Here I say I have amused myself in reading and thinking of my absent Friend, sometimes with a mixture of paine, some-times with pleasure, sometimes anticipating a joy-ful and happy meeting, whilst my Heart would bound and palpitate with the pleasing Idea, and with the purest affection I have held you to my Bosom till my whole Soul had dissolved in Tenderness and my pen fallen from my Hand.

—**Abigail Adams** to John Adams,
29 AUGUST 1776

THERE ARE PERTICULAR TIMES WHEN I FEEL such an uneasiness, such a restlessness, as neither Company, Books, family Cares or any other thing will remove, my Pen is my only pleasure and writing to you the composure of my mind.

—**Abigail Adams** to John Adams,
23 SEPTEMBER 1776

I HAVE OFTEN EXPERIENCED THE WANT OF HIS aid and assistance in the last 3 years of his absence and that Demand increases as our Little ones grow up 3 of whom are sons and at this time of life stand most in need of the joint force of his example and precepts. . . . And can I Sir consent to be seperated from him whom my Heart esteems above all earthly things, and for an unlimited time? My life will be one continued scene of anxiety and apprehension, and must I cheerfully comply with the Demand of my Country?

—**Abigail Adams** to James Lovell,
15 DECEMBER 1777

DIFFICULT AS THE DAY IS, CRUEL AS THIS WAR
has been, seperated as I am on account of it from
the dearest connexion in life, I would not exchange my Country for the Wealth of the Indies,
or be any other than an American tho I might be
Queen or Empress of any Nation upon the
Globe. My Soul is unambitious of pomp or
power. Beneath my Humble roof, Bless'd with
the Society and tenderest affection of my dear
partner, I have enjoyed as much felicity, and as
exquisite happiness as falls to the share of mortals;
and tho I have been calld to sacrifice for my
Country, I can glory in my Sacrifice, and derive
pleasure from my intimate connexion with one
who is esteemed worthy of the important trust
devolved upon him.

　　—**Abigail Adams** to John Adams,
　　18 MAY 1778

IT IS VERY DIFFICULT TO WRITE AT SEA, IN THE
serenest Weather the vessel rolls; and exceeds the
moderate rocking of a cradle, and a calm gives
one more motion, than a Side wind going at 7
and 8 knots an hour. I am now setting in my
State room, which is about 8 foot square, with

two Cabbins, and a chair, which compleatly
fills it, and I write leaning one Arm upon my
cabbin, with a piece of Board in my lap, whilst I
steady myself by holding my other hand upon the
opposite Cabbin; from this you will judge what
accommodations we have for writing. . . . A
sweet Situation for a delicate Lady, but necessity
has no law. . . .

> —**Abigail Adams** to Elizabeth Smith Shaw,
> 10[?] JULY 1784

I HAVE LIVED LONG ENOUGH, AND SEEN ENOUGH
of the world, to check expectations, and to bring
my mind to my circumstances, and retiring to our
own little farm feeding my poultry and improve-
ing my garden has more charms for my fancy,
than residing at the court of Saint James's where I
seldom meet with characters so innofensive as my
Hens and chickings, or minds so well improved as
my garden.

> —**Abigail Adams** to Thomas Jefferson,
> 26 FEBRUARY 1788

[I] DESIRE THEM TO WATCH OVER MY CONDUCT
and if at any time they perceive any alteration in
me with respect to them, arising as they may suppose from my situation in Life, I beg they would
with the utmost freedom acquaint me with it. I
do not feel within myself the least disposition of
the kind, but I know mankind are prone to deceive themselves, and some are disposed to mis-
construe the conduct of those whom they
conceive placed above them.

—**Abigail Adams** to Mary Cranch,
12 JULY 1789

WHY DO YOU SAY THAT YOU FEEL ALONE ON THE
world? I used to think that I felt so too; but,
when I lost my mother, and afterwards my father,
that "alone" appeared to me in a much more for-
midable light. It was like cutting away the main
pillars of a building; and, though no friend can
supply the absence of a good husband, yet, whilst
our parents live, we cannot feel unprotected. To
them we can apply for advice and direction, sure
that it will be given with affection and tenderness.

—**Abigail Adams** to Abigail Adams Smith,
25 JANUARY 1791

Law and the Rule of Law

WHAT A FINE REFLECTION AND CONSOLATION IS
it for a man to reflect that he can be subjected to
no laws, which he does not make himself, or con-
stitute some of his friends to make for him — his
father, brother, neighbor, friend, a man of his
own rank, nearly of his own education, fortune,
habits, passions, prejudices, one whose life and
fortune and liberty are to be affected, like those of
his constituents, by the laws he shall consent to
for himself and them! What a satisfaction is it to
reflect, that he can lie under the imputation of no
guilt, be subjected to no punishment, lose none of
his property, or the necessaries, conveniences, or
ornaments of life, which indulgent Providence has
showered around him: but by the judgment of his
peers, his equals, his neighbors, men who know
him, and to whom he is known; who have no

end to serve by punishing him; who wish to find him innocent, if charged with a crime; and are indifferent, on which side the truth lies, if he disputes with his neighbour!

> —**John Adams,** "Clarendon, No. 3,"
> 27 JANUARY 1766

COUNCIL [I.E., COUNSEL] OUGHT TO BE THE very last thing that an accused Person should want in a free Country.

> —**John Adams,** *Autobiography* (on his decision to act as defense counsel in the Boston Massacre trials)

FACTS ARE STUBBORN THINGS; AND WHATEVER may be our wishes, our inclinations, or the dictates of our passions, they cannot alter the state of facts and evidence.

> —**John Adams,** Summation as chief defense counsel in Boston Massacre trial, 1770

THE DIGNITY AND STABILITY OF GOVERNMENT in all its branches, the morals of the people, and every blessing of society depend so much upon an upright and skillful administration of justice, that the judicial power ought to be distinct from both the legislative and executive, and independent upon both, that so it may be a check upon both, as both should be checks upon that. The judges, therefore, should be always men of learning and experience in the laws, of exemplary morals, great patience, calmness, coolness, and attention. Their minds should not be distracted with jarring interests; they should not be dependent upon any man, or body of men. To these ends, they should hold estates for life in their offices; or, in other words, their commissions should be during good behavior, and their salaries ascertained and established by law. For misbehavior, the grand inquest of the colony, the house of representatives, should impeach them before the governor and council, where they should have time and opportunity to make their defence; but, if convicted, should be removed from their offices, and subjected to such other punishment as shall be thought proper.

—**John Adams,** *Thoughts on Government,*
PHILADELPHIA, 1776

Liberty and Rights

I SAY RIGHTS, FOR SUCH THEY HAVE, UNDOUBT-
edly, antecedent to all earthly government, —
Rights, that cannot be repealed or restrained by
human laws — *Rights,* derived from the great
Legislator of the universe.

> —**John Adams,** "A Dissertation on the
> Canon and Feudal Law," 1765

YOU KNOW MY MIND UPON THIS SUBJECT.
I wish most sincerely there was not a slave in
the province. It allways appeared a most
iniquitous Scheme to me — fight ourselves for
what we are daily robbing and plundering from

those who have as good a right to freedom as
we have.

—**Abigail Adams** to John Adams,
22 SEPTEMBER 1774

I HAVE SOMETIMES BEEN READY TO THINK THAT
the passion for Liberty cannot be Eaquelly Strong
in the Breasts of those who have been accustomed
to deprive their fellow Creatures of theirs.

—**Abigail Adams** to John Adams,
31 MARCH 1776

BUT ALL MEN . . . MUST AGREE, THAT THERE CAN
be no uninterrupted enjoyment of liberty, nor any
good government in society, without laws, or
where standing laws do not govern. . . .

—**John Adams,** *A Defence of the
Constitutions of Government of the United
States . . . ,* 1787–1788

THE RIGHTS OF CONSCIENCE ARE ORIGINAL rights and cannot be alienated; they are the first rights and prescribe the first duties of man, and should be explicitly reserved out of every social compact.

—**John Adams,** marginal note (1790s) on Turgot's letter to Dr. Price, 1778

HAVE YOU EVER FOUND IN HISTORY ONE SINGLE example of a Nation thoroughly Corrupted, that was afterwards restored to Virtue, and without Virtue, there can be no political Liberty.

—**John Adams** to Thomas Jefferson, 21 DECEMBER 1819

Love and Marriage

THERE IS A TYE MORE BINDING THAN HUMANITY and stronger than friendship, which makes us anxious for the happiness and welfare of those to whom it binds us. It makes their misfortunes, sorrows and afflictions our own. . . . By this cord I am not ashamed to own myself bound, nor do I believe that you are wholly free from it.

> —**Abigail Smith** to John Adams,
> 11 AUGUST 1763

HAVE YOU HEARD THE NEWS? THAT TWO Apparitions were seen one evening this week hovering about this house, which very much resembled you and a Cousin of yours. How it should ever enter into the head of an Apparition to assume a form like yours, I cannot devise. When I was told of it I could scarcely believe it, yet I could not declare the contrary, for I did not see it, and therefore had not that demonstration which generally convinces me, that you are not a Ghost.

> —**Abigail Smith** to John Adams,
> 12 SEPTEMBER 1763

YOU CANNOT BE, I KNOW, NOR DO I WISH TO see you an Inactive Spectator, but if the sword be drawn, I bid adieu to all domestick felicity and look forward to that Country where there is nei-ther wars nor rumors of War in a firm belief that thro the Mercy of its Kind we shall both rejoice there together.

> —**Abigail Adams** to John Adams,
> 30 DECEMBER 1773

I WAS PLEASING MYSELF WITH THE THOUGHTS that you would soon be upon your return. Tis in vain to repine. I hope the publick will reap what I sacrifice.

    —**Abigail Adams** to John Adams,
      27 NOVEMBER 1775

I HOPE TO BE MARRIED ONCE MORE MYSELF, IN a few months, to a very amiable lady whom I have inhumanly left a widow in America for nine years, with the exception of a few weeks only. Ask Madame Dumas whether she thinks she has Patriotism enough to consent that you should leave her for nine years pro bono publico [for the public good]? If she has she has another good title to the character of an Heroine.

    —**John Adams** to C. W. F. Dumas,
      16 MAY 1783

Politics and Government

THERE MAY BE OCCASION TO SAY VERY
severe things, before I shall have finished what
I propose, in opposition to this writer, but
there ought to be no reviling. . . . [S]peak out
the whole truth boldly, but use no bad
language.

> —**John Adams,** *Novanglus,*
> 1774–1775

I HAVE SAID, THAT THE PRACTICE OF FREE
governments alone can be quoted with propriety
to show the sense of nations. But the sense and
practice of nations is not enough. Their practice

must be reasonable, just, and right, or it will not govern Americans.

    —**John Adams,** *Novanglus,*
      1774–1775

WHEN A GREAT QUESTION IS FIRST STARTED, there are very few, even of the greatest minds, which suddenly and intuitively comprehend it, in all its consequences.

    —**John Adams,** *Novanglus,*
      1774–1775

THERE IS NO AVOIDING ALL INCONVENIENCES in human affairs.

    —**John Adams,** *Novanglus,*
      1774–1775

IT IS IN VAIN TO EXPECT OR HOPE TO CARRY ON government, against the universal bent and genius of the people; we may whimper and whine as much as we will, but nature made it impossible, when she made men.

—**John Adams,** *Novanglus,*
1774–1775

TIS UNHAPPY THAT IN THE INFANCY OF OUR republicks such unworthy characters should stain our Anals and Lessen us in the Eyes of foreign powers. Yet this will ever be the case where self Interest is more powerful than publick virtue.

—**Abigail Adams** to Mercy Otis Warren,
22 JANUARY 1779

THE SCIENCE OF GOVERNMENT IT IS MY DUTY to study, more than all other Sciences: the Art of Legislation and Administration and Negotiation, ought to take Place, indeed to exclude in a manner all other Arts. — I must study Politicks and War that my sons may have liberty to study Mathematicks and Philosophy. My sons ought to study Mathematicks and Philosophy, Geography,

natural History, Naval Architecture, navigation,
Commerce and Agriculture, in order to give their
Children a right to study Painting, Poetry,
Musick, Architecture, Statuary, Tapestry and
Porcelaine.

—**John Adams** to Abigail Adams, after
12 MAY 1780

I HAVE THE HONOR AND CONSOLATION TO BE
a republican on principle, that is to say, I esteem
that form of government the best of which
human nature is capable. Almost everything that
is estimable in civil life has originated under such
governments. Two republican powers, Athens
and Rome, have done more honour to our
species than all the rest of it. . . . I am not, however, an enthusiast who wishes to overturn em-
pires and monarchies for the sake of introducing
republican forms of government, and therefore, I
am no King-killer, King-hater, or King-despiser.

—**John Adams** to the Marquis de Lafayette,
21 MAY 1782

IT IS NOT TO FLATTER THE PASSIONS OF THE PEOPLE, to be sure, nor is it the way to obtain a present enthusiastic popularity, to tell them that in a single assembly they will act as arbitrarily and tyrannically as any despot, but it is a sacred truth, and as demonstrable as any proposition whatever, that a sovereignty in a single assembly must necessarily and will certainly be exercised by a majority, as tyrannically as any sovereignty was ever exercised by kings or nobles. And if a balance of passions and interests is not scientifically concerted, the present struggle in Europe will be little beneficial to mankind, and produce nothing but another thousand years of feudal fanaticism, under new and strange names.

> —John Adams to the Marquis de Lafayette, 21 MAY 1782

IT MUST BE ACKNOWLEDGED THAT EVERY example of a government, which has a large mixture of democratical power, exhibits something to our view which is amiable, noble, and I had almost said, divine.

> —John Adams, *A Defence of the Constitutions of Government of the United States . . . ,* 1787–1788

WHEN WRITERS ON LEGISLATION HAVE RECOURSE
to poetry, their images may be beautiful, but they
prove nothing.

> —**John Adams,** *A Defence of the
> Constitutions of Government of the United
> States . . . ,* 1787–1788

DECLAMATORY FLOURISHES, ALTHOUGH THEY
may furnish a mob with watchwords, afford no
reasonable conviction to the understanding.

> —**John Adams,** *A Defence of the
> Constitutions of Government of the United
> States . . . ,* 1787–1788

ALL NATIONS, FROM THE BEGINNING, HAVE BEEN
agitated by the same passions. The principles de-
veloped here will go a great way in explaining
every phenomenon that occurs in the history of
government. The vegetable and animal kingdoms,
and those heavenly bodies whose existence and

movements we are as yet only permitted faintly to perceive, do not appear to be governed by laws more uniform or certain than those which regulate the moral and political world.

>   —John Adams, *A Defence of the Constitutions of Government of the United States . . . ,* 1787–1788

OTHERS, AGAIN, MORE RATIONALLY, DEFINE A republic to signify only a government, in which all men, rich and poor, magistrates and subjects, officers and people, masters and servants, the first citizen and the last, are equally subject to the laws. This, indeed, appears to be the true and only true definition of a republic.

>   —John Adams, *A Defence of the Constitutions of Government of the United States . . . ,* 1787–1788

THE PEOPLE ARE THE FOUNTAIN AND ORIGINAL of the power of kings and lords, governors and

senates, as well as the house of commons, or assembly of representatives. And if the people are
sufficiently enlightened to see all the dangers that
surround them, they will always be represented
by a distinct personage to manage the whole executive power; a distinct senate, to be guardians of
property against levellers for the purposes of plun-
der, to be a repository of the national tradition of
public maxims, customs, and manners, and to be
controllers, in turn, both of kings and their minis-
ters on one side, and the representatives of the
people on the other, when either discover a disposition to do wrong; and a distinct house of representatives, to be the guardians of the public
purse, and to protect the people, in their turn,
against both kings and nobles.

> —John Adams, *A Defence of the
> Constitutions of Government of the United
> States . . . ,* 1787–1788

ELECTIONS, MY DEAR SIR, ELECTIONS TO OFFICES
which are great objects of Ambition, I look at
with terror. Experiments of this kind have been
so often tryed, and so universally found produc-

tive of Horrors, that there is great Reason to
dread them.

—**John Adams** to Thomas Jefferson,
6 DECEMBER 1787

ALL EUROPE RESOUNDS WITH PROJECTS FOR
reviving, States and Assemblies, I think, and
France is taking the lead. — How such assemblies
will mix, with Simple Monarchies, is the question. Superstition, Bigotry, Ignorance, Imposture,
Tyranny and Misery must be lessened somewhat.
— But I fancy it will be found somewhat difficult,
to conduct and regulate these debates. . . . The
world will be entertained with noble sentiments
and enchanting Eloquence, but will not essential
Ideas be sometimes forgotten, in the anxious
study of Brilliant Phrases? . . . Corrections and
Reformations are much wanted in all the
Institutions of Europe Ecclesiastical and civil: but
how or when they will be made is not easy to
guess. — It would be folly I think to do no more
than try over again Experiments, that have been
already a million times tryed. Attempts to recon-
cile Contradictions will not succed, and to think
of Reinstituting Republicks, as absurdly consti-

tuted as were the most which the world has seen, would be to revive Confusion and Carnage, which must again End in Despotism.

—**John Adams** to Thomas Jefferson,
10 DECEMBER 1787

POWER NATURALLY GROWS. WHY? BECAUSE human passions are insatiable. But that power alone can grow which already is too great; that which is unchecked; that which has no equal power to control it.

—**John Adams** to Roger Sherman,
18 JULY 1789

NATURE HAS TAKEN EFFECTUAL CARE OF HER own work. She has wrought the passions into the texture and essence of the soul, and has not left it in the power of art to destroy them. To regulate and not to eradicate them is the province of policy. It is of the highest importance to education, to life, and to society, not only that they should not be destroyed, but that they should be grati-

fied, encouraged, and arranged on the side of
virtue.

>—**John Adams,** *Discourses on Davila,*
>   1790–1791

I AM A MORTAL AND IRRECONCILABLE ENEMY
to monarchy. I am no friend to hereditary limited
monarchy in America. This I know can never be
admitted without an hereditary Senate to control
it, and a hereditary nobility or Senate I know to
be unattainable and impracticable. I should
scarcely be for it, if it were.

>—**John Adams** to Benjamin Rush,
>   18 APRIL 1790

IF YOU SUPPOSE THAT I HAVE OR EVER HAD
a design or desire, of atempting to introduce a
Government of King, Lords and Commons, or
in other Words an hereditary Executive, or an
hereditary Senate, either into the Government
of the United States or that of any Individual
State, in this Country, you are wholly mistaken.

There is not such a Thought expressed or intimated in any public writing or private Letter of mine, and I may safely challenge all Mankind to produce such a passage and quote the Chapter and Verse.

> —**John Adams** to Thomas Jefferson,
>   29 JULY 1791

[P]OLITICIANS SHOULD OPEN THEIR EYES UPON the empty illusions by which they have been cheated by soldiers, by priests, by merchants, by mechanics, and even by husbandmen and shepherds. Politicians are cheated as often as they cheat, and the way to improve society and reform the world is to enlighten men, spread knowledge, and convince the multitude that they have, or may have, sense, knowledge, and virtue. Declamations against the cunning of politicians and the ignorance, folly, inconstancy or effrontery of the multitude will never do it.

> —**John Adams,** marginal note (1790s) on
>   Turgot's letter to Dr. Price, 1778

[M]Y COUNTRY HAS IN ITS WISDOM CONTRIVED for me the most insignificant office [the vice presidency] that ever the invention of man contrived or his imagination conceived. And as I can do neither good nor evil, I must be borne away by others, and meet the common fate.

—**John Adams** to Abigail Adams,
19 DECEMBER 1793

CORRUPTION IN ELECTIONS HAS HERETOFORE destroyed all Elective Governments. What Regulations or Precautions may be devised to prevent it in future, I am content with you to leave to Posterity to consider. You and I shall go to the Kingdom of the just or at least shall be released from the Republick of the Unjust, with Hearts pure and hands clean of all Corruption in Elections; so much I firmly believe. Those who shall introduce the foul Fiend on the Stage, after We are gone must exorcise him as they can.

—**John Adams** to Thomas Jefferson,
6 APRIL 1796

CAN AUTHORITY BE MORE AMIABLE AND respectable when it descends from accidents or institutions established in remote antiquity than when it springs fresh from the hearts and judgments of an honest and enlightened people? For it is the people only that are represented. It is their power and majesty that is reflected, and only for their good, in every legitimate government, under whatever form it may appear. The existence of such a government as ours for any length of time is a full proof of a general dissemination of knowledge and virtue throughout the whole body of the people. And what object or consideration more pleasing than this can be presented to the human mind? If national pride is ever justifiable or excusable it is when it springs, not from power or riches, grandeur or glory, but from conviction of national innocence, information, and benevolence.

— **John Adams,** Inaugural Address,
4 MARCH 1797

WE WANT MORE MEN OF *DEEDS,* AND FEWER of words — a speech which space take[s] up ten collums of a newspaper and part of an additional

supplement must contain very weighty and important matter indeed to induce people to hear it
patiently, or read it afterward.

> —**Abigail Adams** to William Smith,
>   19 JULY 1797

I PRAY HEAVEN TO BESTOW THE BEST OF
Blessings on this House and all that shall hereafter
inhabit it. May none but honest and wise Men
ever rule under this roof.

> —**John Adams** to Abigail Adams,
>   2 NOVEMBER 1800 (referring to the
>   Executive Mansion, now known
>   as the White House; this passage is
>   carved on a mantelpiece in the
>   East Room.)

THAT SOME RESTRAINT SHOULD BE LAID UPON
the asassin, who stabs reputation, all civilized
Nations have assented to. In no Country has
calumny falshood and revileing stalked abroad
more licentiously, than in this. No political

Character has been secure from its attacks, no reputation so fair, as not to be wounded by it, untill truth and falshood lie in one undistinguished heap. If there are no checks to be resorted to in the Laws of the Land, will not Man become the judge and avenger of his own wrongs, and as in a late instance, the sword and the pistol decide the contest?

> —**Abigail Adams** to Thomas Jefferson,
> 18 AUGUST 1804

I LOVE THE PEOPLE OF AMERICA AND BELIEVE them to be incapable of ingratitude. They have been, they may be, and they are deceived. It is the duty of somebody to undeceive them.

> —**John Adams** to Benjamin Rush,
> 27 FEBRUARY 1805

I LOOK AT THE PRESIDENTIAL ELECTION AS I DO at the squabbles of little girls about their dolls and at the more serious wrangles of little boys, which sometimes come to blows, about their rattles and whistles. It will be a mighty bustle about a mighty bauble.

—**John Adams** to Benjamin Rush,
25 JULY 1808

LEGISLATORS! BEWARE HOW YOU MAKE LAWS TO shock the prejudices or break the habits of the people. Innovations even of the most certain and obvious utility must be introduced with great caution, prudence, and skill.

—**John Adams** to Benjamin Rush,
14 MARCH 1809

THE CLOCK WOULD BE MORE SIMPLE IF YOU destroyed all the wheels and left only the weights or the spring, but it would not tell the time of day. A farmer's barn would be more simple if without apartments and he turned in all together his horses, cattle, sheep and hogs: yet his haymows would be wasted and his stock killed and gored. A ship would be more simple without a rudder, with but one mast and but one sail. A city would be more simple if you built it all in one house or barrack without departments and turned all the people in together. The solar system would be more simple if all the planets were destroyed and you left only the sun. The universe would be more simple if it were all in one globe. The earth would be more simple if it were all fire, water, air or earth, but its inhabitants must perish in either case. The laws would be more simple if all reduced to one 'Be it enacted that every man, woman and child shall do their duty.' It is silly to be eternally harping upon simplicity in a form of government. The simplest of all possible governments is a despotism in one. Simplicity is not the summum bonum [highest good].

> —**John Adams,** marginal note (1812) on Mary Wollstonecraft, *Historical and Moral View of the Origin and Progress of the French Revolution,* 1794

THE REAL TERRORS OF BOTH PARTIES HAVE allways been, and now are, The fear that they shall loose the Elections and consequently the Loaves and Fishes; and that their Antagonists will obtain them. Both parties have excited artificial

Terrors and if I were summoned as a Witness to say upon Oath, which Party had excited, Machiavillialy, the most terror, and which had really felt the most, I could not give a more sincere Answer, than in the vulgar Style, "Put Them in a bagg and shake them, and then see which comes out first."

> —**John Adams** to Thomas Jefferson, 30 JUNE 1813

WHILE ALL OTHER SCIENCES HAVE ADVANCED, that of Government is at a stand; little better understood; little better practiced now than 3 or 4 thousand Years ago. What is the Reason? I say Parties and Factions will not suffer, or permit Improvements to be made. As soon as one Man hints at an improvement his Rival opposes it. No sooner has one Party discovered or invented an Amelioration of the Condition of Man or the order of Society, than the opposite Party, belies it, misconstrues it, ridicules it, insults it, and persecutes it. Records are destroyed. Histories are annihilated or interpolated, or prohibited sometimes by Popes, sometimes by Emperors, sometimes by

Aristocratical and sometimes by democratical Assemblies and sometimes by Mobs.

—**John Adams** to Thomas Jefferson,
9 JULY 1813

PICK UP, THE FIRST 100 MEN YOU MEET, AND make a Republick. Every Man will have an equal Vote. But when deliberations and discussions are opened it will be found that 25, by their Talents, Virtues being equal, will be able to carry 50 Votes. Every one of these 25, is an Aristocrat, in my Sense of the Word; whether he obtains his one Vote in Addition to his own, by his Birth Fortune, Figure, Eloquence, Science, learning, Craft Cunning, or even his Character for good fellowship and a bon vivant.

—**John Adams** to Thomas Jefferson,
15 NOVEMBER 1813

I WILL TELL YOU IN A FEW WORDS WHAT I MEAN by an aristocrat, and, consequently, what I mean

by aristocracy. By an aristocrat, I mean every man
who can command or influence TWO VOTES,
ONE BESIDES HIS OWN.

—**John Adams** to John Taylor,
[?] APRIL 1814

THE FUNDAMENTAL ARTICLE OF MY POLITICAL
Creed is, that Despotism, or unlimited
Sovereignty, or absolute Power is the same in a
Majority of a popular Assembly, an Aristocratical
Council, an Oligarchical Junto and a single
Emperor. Equally arbitrary cruel bloody and in
every respect diabolical.

—**John Adams** to Thomas Jefferson,
13 NOVEMBER 1815

YOU ASK, HOW IT HAS HAPPENED THAT ALL
Europe, has acted on the Principle "that Power
was Right." I know not what Answer to give
you, but this, that Power always, sincerely, consci-
entiously . . . believes itself Right. Power always
thinks it has a great Soul, and vast Views, beyond

the Comprehension of the Weak, and that it is
doing God Service, when it is violating all his
Laws. Our Passions, Ambition, Avarice, Love,
Resentment etc possess so much metaphysical
Subtilty and so much overpowering Eloquence,
that they insinuate themselves into the
Understanding and the Conscience and convert
both to their Party. And I may be deceived as
much as any of them, when I say, that Power
must never be trusted without a Check.

   —John Adams to Thomas Jefferson,
    2 FEBRUARY 1816

Religion

THE DESIGNS OF PROVIDENCE ARE INSCRUTABLE.
It affords conjunctures, favorable for their designs,
to bad men, as well as to good.

> —**John Adams,** *Novanglus,*
> 1774–1775

[W]HAT DO WE MEAN BY THE IDEAS, THE
thoughts, the reason, the intelligence, or the
speech of God? His intelligence is a subject too
vast, too incomprehensible for Plato, Philo, Paul
or Peter, Jews, Gentiles or Christians. Let us
adore, not presume nor dogmatize. Even the
great Teacher may not reveal this subject. There
never was, is not, and never will be more than
one Being in the universe capable of compre-
hending it. At least this is the humble and adoring

opinion of the writer of this note. . . . Admire and adore the Author of the telescopic universe, love and esteem the work, do all in your power to lessen ill, and increase good: but never assume to comprehend.

> —**John Adams,** marginal note on Joseph Priestley, *Early Opinions Concerning Jesus Christ*

WAS THERE EVER A POPULAR RELIGION THAT DID not pretend to divine instruction? . . . Was there ever a country, in which philosophers, politicians, and theologians believed what they taught to the vulgar?

> —**John Adams,** marginal note on Joseph Priestley, *Early Opinions Concerning Jesus Christ*

BIGOTRY, SUPERSTITION, AND ENTHUSIASM ON religious subjects I have long since set at defiance. I have attended public worship in all countries and with all sects and believe them all much better than no religion, though I have not thought myself obliged to believe all I heard. Religion I hold to be essential to morals; I never read of an irreligious character in Greek or Roman history, nor in any other history, nor have I known one in life, who was not a rascal. Name one if you can, living or dead.

—**John Adams** to Benjamin Rush,
  18 APRIL 1808

THE TEN COMMANDMENTS AND THE SERMON ON the Mount contain my religion.

—**John Adams** to Thomas Jefferson,
  4 NOVEMBER 1816

FOR THE LAST YEAR OR TWO I HAVE DEVOTED myself to this kind of Study [i.e., of history of religion]. . . . Romances all! I have learned nothing of importance to me, for they have made no Change in my moral or religious Creed, which has for 50 or 60 years been contained in four

short Words *"Be just and good."* In this result they
all agree with me.

      —John Adams to Thomas Jefferson,
        12 DECEMBER 1816

TWENTY TIMES, IN THE COURSE OF MY LATE
Reading, have I been upon the point of
breaking out, 'This would be the best of all
possible Worlds, if there were no Religion in
it.'!!! But in this exclamation I should have been
as fanatical as Bryant or Cleverly. Without
Religion this World would be Something not
fit to be mentioned in polite Company, I mean
Hell. So far from believing in the total and
universal depravity of human Nature, I believe
there is no Individual totally depraved. The most
abandoned Scoundrel that ever existed, never
Yet Wholly extinguished his Conscience, and
while Conscience remains there is some
Religion.

      —John Adams to Thomas Jefferson,
        19 APRIL 1817

WE THINK OURSELVES POSSESSED OR AT LEAST
we boast that we are so of Liberty of conscience
on all subjects and of the right of free inquiry and
private judgment, in all cases and yet how far are
we from these exalted privileges in fact. There
exists I believe throughout the whole Christian
world a law which makes it blasphemy to deny or
to doubt the divine inspiration of all the books of
the old and new Testaments from Genesis to
Revelations. . . . Now what free inquiry when a
writer must surely encounter the risk of fine or
imprisonment for adducing any arguments for investigation into the divine authority of those
books? . . . I think such laws a great embarrass-
ment, great obstructions to the improvement of
the human mind. Books that cannot bear examination certainly ought not to be established as divine inspiration by penal laws. It is true few
persons appear desirous to put such laws in execution and it is also true that some few persons
are hardy enough to venture to depart from
them; but as long as they continue in force as laws
the human mind must make an awkward and
clumsy progress in its investigations. I wish they
were repealed. The substance and essence of
Christianity as I understand it is eternal and un-
changeable and will bear examination forever but

it has been mixed with extraneous ingredients which I think will not bear examination and they ought to be separated.

      —John Adams to Thomas Jefferson,
        23 JANUARY 1825

War and Peace

I BELIEVE WITH YOU THAT WARS ARE THE natural and unavoidable effects of the constitution of human nature and the fabric of the globe it is destined to inhabit and to rule. I believe further that wars, at times, are as necessary for the preservation and perfection, the prosperity, liberty, happiness, virtue, and independence of nations as gales of wind to the salubrity of the atmosphere, or the agitations of the ocean to prevent its stagnation and putrefaction. As I believe this to be the constitution of God Almighty and the constant order of his Providence, I must esteem all the speculations of divines and philosophers about universal and perpetual peace as shortsighted, frivolous romances.

—**John Adams** to Benjamin Rush,
7 JULY 1812

National defense is one of the cardinal duties of a statesman. On this head I recollect nothing with which to reproach myself. The subject has always been near my heart. The delightful imagination of universal and perpetual peace have often amused, but have never been credited by me.

　　—John Adams to James Lloyd,
　　　　JANUARY 1815

Women

WOMEN YOU KNOW SIR ARE CONSIDERD AS
Domestick Beings, and altho they inherit an
Eaquel Share of curiosity with the other Sex,
yet but few are hardy eno' to venture abroad,
and explore the amazing variety of distant Lands.
The Natural tendencies and Delicacy of our
Constitutions, added to the many Dangers we are
subject too from your Sex, renders it almost im-
posible for a Single Lady to travel without injury
to her character.

      —Abigail Adams to Isaac Smith,
        20 APRIL 1771

I LONG TO HEAR THAT YOU HAVE DECLARED AN
independancy — and by the way in the new Code
of Laws which I suppose it will be necessary for
you to make I desire you would Remember the

Ladies, and be more generous and favourable to
them than your ancestors. Do not put such unlimited power into the hands of the Husbands.
Remember all Men would be tyrants if they
could. If perticular care and attention is not paid
to the Ladies we are determined to foment a
Rebelion, and will not hold ourselves bound by
any Laws in which we have no voice, or
Representation.

That your Sex are Naturally Tyrannical is a
Truth so thoroughly established as to admit of
no dispute, but such of you as wish to be happy
willingly give up the harsh title of Master for
the more tender and endearing one of Friend.
Why then, not put it out of the power of the
vicious and the Lawless to use us with cruelty
and indignity with impunity. Men of sense in
all Ages abhor those customs which treat us
only as the vassals of your sex. Regard us then
as Beings placed by providence under your
protection and in immitation of the Supreme
Being make use of that power only for our
happiness.

> **—Abigail Adams** to John Adams,
>   31 MARCH 1776

In America . . . so few Ladies have a taste for
Historick knowledge, that even their own
Country was not much known to them until the
present Revolution.

> —**Abigail Adams** to John Adams,
>   3 FEBRUARY 1781

I CANNOT SAY THAT I THINK YOU VERY
generous to the Ladies, for whilst you are
proclaiming peace and good will to Men,
Emancipating all Nations, you insist upon retain-
ing an absolute power over Wives. But you must
remember that Arbitrary power is like most other
things which are very hard, very liable to be bro-
ken — and notwithstanding all your wise Laws
and Maxims we have it in our power not only to
free ourselves but to subdue our Masters, and
without violence throw both your natural and
legal authority at our feet

"Charm by accepting, by submitting sway
yet have our Humour most when we obey."

> —**Abigail Adams** to John Adams,
>   7 MAY 1776

I HAVE SOMETIMES THOUGHT THAT WE ARE
formed to experience more exquisite Sensations
than is the Lot of your Sex. More tender and sus-
ceptible by Nature of those impressions which
create happiness or misery, we Suffer and enjoy in
a higher degree. I never wondered at the philosopher who thanked the Gods that he was created a
Man rather than a Woman.

> —**Abigail Adams** to John Adams,
>   10 APRIL 1782

PATRIOTISM IN THE FEMALE SEX IS THE MOST
disinterested of all virtues. Excluded from honours
and from offices, we cannot attach ourselves to
the State or Government from having held a
place of Eminence. Even in the freest countrys
our property is subject to the controul and disposition of our partners, to whom the Laws have
given a Sovereign Authority. Deprived of a voice
in Legislation, obliged to submit to those Laws
which are imposed upon us, is it not sufficient to
make us indifferent to the Publick Welfare? Yet all

History and every age exhibit Instances of patri-
otick virtue in the female Sex; which considering
our situation equals the most Heroick of yours.

   —Abigail Adams to John Adams,
      17 JUNE 1782

THOUGHTS ON GOVERNMENT:
Applicable to the Present State of the American Colonies.
In a Letter from a Gentleman to His Friend
Philadelphia:
John Dunlap, 1776.

My dear Sir,

If I was equal to the task of forming a plan for the government of a colony, I should be flattered with your request, and very happy to comply with it; because, as the divine science of politicks is the science of social happiness, and the blessings of society depend entirely on the constitutions of government, which are generally institutions that last for many generations, there can be no employment more agreeable to a benevolent mind than a research after the best. Pope flattered tyrants too much when he said,

"For forms of government let fools contest,
  That which is best administered is best."[1]

Nothing can be more fallacious than this: But poets read history to collect flowers, not fruits — they attend to fanciful images, not the effects of social institutions. Nothing is more certain from the history of nations, and the nature of man, than that some forms of government are better fitted for being well administered than others.

WE ought to consider, what is the end of government, before we determine which is the best form. — Upon this point all speculative politicians will agree, that the happiness of society is the end of government, as all Divines and moral Philosophers will agree that the happiness of the individual is the end of man. From this principle it will follow, that the form of government, which communicates ease, comfort, security, or in one word happiness to the greatest number of persons, and in the greatest degree, is the best.

ALL sober inquirers after truth, ancient and modern, Pagan and Christian, have declared that the happiness of man, as well as his dignity, consists in virtue. Confucius, Zoroaster, Socrates, Mahomet, not to mention authorities really sacred, have agreed in this.

IF there is a form of government then, whose

principle and foundation is virtue, will not every sober man acknowledge it better calculated to promote the general happiness than any other form?

FEAR is the foundation of most governments; but is so sordid and brutal a passion, and renders men, in whose breasts it predominates, so stupid, and miserable, that Americans will not be likely to approve of any political institution which is founded on it.

HONOUR is truly sacred, But holds a lower rank in the scale of moral excellence than virtue. — Indeed, the former is but a part of the latter, and consequently has not equal pretensions to support a frame of government productive of human happiness.

THE foundation of every government is some principle or passion in the minds of the people. — The noblest principles and most generous affections in our nature then, have the fairest chance to support the noblest and most generous models of government.

A MAN must be indifferent to the sneers of modern Englishmen to mention in their company, the names of Sidney, Harrington, Locke, Milton, Nedham, Neville, Burnet, and Hoadly.[2] — No small fortitude is necessary to confess that one has read them. The wretched condition of this country, however, for ten or fifteen years past, has frequently reminded me of their principles and reasonings. They will convince any candid mind, that there is no good government but what is Republican. That the only valuable part of the British constitution is so; because the very definition of a Republic is "an Empire of Laws, and not of men." That, as a Republic is the best of governments, so that particular arrangement of the powers of society, or in other words that form of government, which is best contrived to secure an impartial and exact execution of the laws, is the best of Republics.

OF Republics, there is an inexhaustible variety, because the possible combinations of the powers of society, are capable of innumerable variations.

AS good government, is an empire of laws, how shall your laws be made? In a large society, inhabiting an extensive country, it is impossible that the whole should assemble, to make laws: The first necessary step then, is, to depute power from the many, to a few of the most wise and good. — But by what rules shall you choose your Representatives? Agree upon the number and qualifications of persons, who shall have the benefit of choosing, or annex this privilege to the inhabitants of a certain extent of ground.

THE principal difficulty lies, and the greatest

care should be employed, in constituting this Representative Assembly. It should be in miniature, an exact portrait of the people at large. It should think, feel, reason, and act like them. That it may be the interest of this Assembly to do strict justice at all times, it should be an equal representation, or in other words equal interest among the people should have equal interest in it. — Great care should be taken to effect this, and to prevent unfair, partial, and corrupt elections. Such regulations, however, may be better made in times of greater tranquillity than the present, and they will spring up themselves naturally, when all the powers of government come to be in the hands of the people's friends. At present it will be safest to proceed in all established modes to which the people have been familiarised by habit.

A REPRESENTATION of the people in one assembly being obtained, a question arises, whether all the powers of government, legislative, executive, and judicial, shall be left in this body? I think a people cannot be long free, nor ever happy, whose government is in one Assembly. My reasons for this opinion are as follow.

1. A SINGLE assembly is liable to all the vices, follies, and frailties of an individual. — Subject to fits of humor, starts of passion, flights of enthusiasm, partialities of prejudice, and consequently

productive of hasty results and absurd judgments: And all these errors ought to be cor-
rected and defects supplied by some controuling
power.

2. A SINGLE assembly is apt to be avaricious, and
in time will not scruple to exempt itself from
burthens which it will lay, without compunc-
tion, on its constituents.

3. A SINGLE assembly is apt to grow ambitious,
and after a time will not hesitate to vote itself
perpetual. This was one fault of the long
parliament, but more remarkably of Holland,
whose Assembly first voted themselves from
annual to septennial, then for life, and after a
course of years, that all vacancies happening by
death, or otherwise, should be filled by themselves, without any application to constituents
at all.

4. A REPRESENTATIVE assembly, altho' extremely
well qualified, and absolutely necessary as a
branch of the legislative, is unfit to exercise the
executive power, for want of two essential
properties, secrecy and dispatch.

5. A REPRESENTATIVE assembly is still less
qualified for the judicial power; because it is
too numerous, too slow, and too little skilled
in the laws.

6. BECAUSE a single assembly, possessed of all the

powers of government, would make arbitrary laws for their own interest, execute all laws arbitrarily for their own interest, and adjudge all controversies in their own favour.

BUT shall the whole power of legislation rest in one Assembly? Most of the foregoing reasons apply equally to prove that the legislative power ought to be more complex — to which we may add, that if the legislative power is wholly in one Assembly, and the executive in another, or in a single person, these two powers will oppose and enervate upon each other, until the contest shall end in war, and the whole power, legislative and executive, be usurped by the strongest.

THE judicial power, in such case, could not mediate, or hold the balance between the two contending powers, because the legislative would undermine it. — And this shows the necessity too, of giving the executive power a negative upon the legislative, otherwise this will be continually encroaching upon that.

TO avoid these dangers, let a distinct assembly be constituted, as a mediator between the two extreme branches of the legislature, that which represents the people, and that which is vested with the executive power.

LET the Representative Assembly then elect by ballot, from among themselves or their constituents, or both, a distinct Assembly, which, for the sake of perspicuity we will call a Council. It may consist of any number you please, say twenty or thirty, and should have a free and independent exercise of its judgment, and consequently a negative voice in the legislature.

THESE two bodies thus constituted, and made integral parts of the legislature, let them unite, and by joint ballot choose a Governor, who, after being stripped of most of those badges of domination called prerogatives, should have a free and independent exercise of his judgment, and be made also an integral part of the legislature. This I know is liable to objections, and, if you please you may make him only President of the Council, as in Connecticut: But as the Governor is to be invested with the executive power, with consent of Council, I think he ought to have a negative upon the legislative. If he is annually elective, as he ought to be, he will always have so much reverence and affection for the People, their Representatives and Councillors, that although you give him an independent exercise of his judgment, he will seldom use it in opposition to the two houses, except in cases the public utility of which would be conspicuous, and some such cases would happen.

IN the present exigency of American affairs,

when, by an act of Parliament we are put out of
the royal protection, and consequently discharged
from our allegiance; and it has become necessary
to assume government for our immediate security,
the Governor, Lieutenant-Governor, Secretary,
Treasurer, Commissary, Attorney-General, should
be chosen by joint ballot, of both Houses. And
these and all other elections, especially of
Representatives and Councillors, should be annual, there not being in the whole circle of the
sciences, a maxim more infallible than this,
"where annual elections end, there slavery
begins."

THESE great men, in this respect, should be,
once a year

"Like bubbles on the sea of matter borne,
They rise, they break, and to that sea return."[3]

This will teach them the great political virtues
of humility, patience, and moderation, without
which every man in power becomes a ravenous
beast of prey.

THIS mode of constituting the great offices of
state will answer very well for the present, but if,
by experiment, it should be found inconvenient,
the legislature may at its leisure devise other
methods of creating them, by elections of the
people at large, as in Connecticut, or it may

enlarge the term for which they shall be chosen to seven years, or three years, or for life, or make any other alterations which the society shall find productive of its ease, its safety, its freedom, or in one word, its happiness.

A ROTATION of all offices, as well as of Representatives and Councillors, has many advocates, and is contended for with many plausible arguments. It would be attended no doubt with many advantages; and if the society has a sufficient number of suitable characters to supply the great number of vacancies which would be made by such a rotation, I can see no objection to it. These persons may be allowed to serve for three years, and then be excluded three years, or for any longer or shorter term.

ANY seven or nine of the legislative Council may be made a Quorum, for doing business as a Privy Council, to advise the Governor in the exercise of the executive branch of power, and in all acts of state.

THE GOVERNOR should have the command of the militia, and of all your armies. The power of pardons should be with the Governor and Council.

JUDGES, justices, and all other officers, civil and military, should be nominated and appointed by the Governor, with the advice and consent of

Council, unless you choose to have a government more popular; if you do, all officers, civil and military, may be chosen by joint ballot of both Houses, or in order to preserve the independence and importance of each House, by ballot of one House, concurred in by the other. Sheriffs should be chosen by the freeholders of counties — so should Registers of Deeds and Clerks of Counties.

ALL officers should have commissions, under the hand of the Governor and seal of the Colony.

THE dignity and stability of government in all its branches, the morals of the people and every blessing of society, depends so much upon an upright and skillful administration of justice, that the judicial power ought to be distinct from both the legislative and executive, and independent upon both, that so it may be a check upon both, as both should be checks upon that. The Judges therefore should be always men of learning and experience in the laws, of exemplary morals, great patience, calmness, coolness, and attention. Their minds should not be distracted with jarring interests; they should not be dependent upon any man, or body of men. To these ends they should hold estates for life in their offices; or in other words their commissions should be during good behaviour, and their salaries ascertained and established by law. For misbehaviour the grand inquest of the Colony, the House of Representatives, should impeach them before the Governor and Council, where they should have time and opportunity to make their defence, but if convicted should be removed from their offices, and subjected to such other punishment as shall be thought proper.

A MILITIA LAW, requiring all men, or with very few exceptions, besides cases of conscience, to be provided with arms and ammunition, to be trained at certain seasons; and requiring counties, towns, or other small districts to be provided with public stocks of ammunition and entrenching utensils, and with some settled plans for transporting provisions after the militia, when marched to defend their country against sudden invasions; and requiring certain districts to be provided with field pieces, companies of matrosses, and perhaps some regiments of light horse, is always a wise institution, and in the present circumstances of our country indispensable.

LAWS for the liberal education of youth, especially of the lower class of people, are so extremely wise and useful, that, to a humane and generous mind, no expence for this purpose would be thought extravagant.

THE very mention of sumptuary laws will excite a smile. Whether our countrymen have wisdom and virtue enough to submit to them I know not. But the happiness of the people might be greatly promoted by them, and a revenue saved sufficient to carry on this war forever. Frugality is a great revenue, besides curing us of vanities, levities and fopperies, which are real antidotes to all great, manly and warlike virtues.

BUT must not all commissions run in the name of a King? No. Why may they not as well run thus, "The Colony of to A. B. greeting," and be [attested] by the Governor?

WHY may not writs, instead of running in the name of the King, run thus, "The Colony of [ ] to the Sheriff," &c., and be [attested] by the Chief Justice?

WHY may not indictments conclude, "against the peace of the Colony of [ ] and the dignity of the same?"

A CONSTITUTION, founded on these principles, introduces know ledge among the People, and inspires them with a conscious dignity, becoming Freemen. A general emulation takes place, which causes good humor, sociability, good manners, and good morals to be general. That elevation of sentiment, inspired by such a government, makes the common people brave and enterprizing. That ambition which is inspired by it makes them sober, industrious and frugal. You will find among them some elegance, perhaps, but more solidity; a little pleasure, but a great deal of business — some politeness, but more civility. If you compare such a country with the regions of domination, whether Monarchical or Aristocratical, you will fancy yourself in Arcadia or Elisium.

IF the Colonies should assume governments separately, they should be left entirely to their own choice of the forms, and if a Continental Constitution should be formed, it should be a Congress, containing a fair and adequate Representation of the Colonies, and its authority should sacredly be confined to these cases, viz., war, trade, disputes between Colony and Colony, the Post-Office, and the unappropriated lands of the Crown, as they used to be called.

THESE COLONIES, under such forms of government, and in such a union, would be un-conquerable by all the Monarchies of Europe.

You and I, my dear Friend, have been sent into life, at a time when the greatest lawgivers of an-tiquity would have wished to have lived. — How few of the human race have ever enjoyed an op-portunity of making an election of government more than of air, soil, or climate, for themselves or their children! — When! Before the present epocha, had three millions of people full power and a fair opportunity to form and establish the wisest and happiest government that human wisdom can contrive? I hope you will avail yourself and your country of that extensive learning and indefatigable industry which you possess, to assist her in the formation of the happiest governments, and the best character of a great people. For myself, I must beg you to keep my name out of sight; for this feeble attempt, if it should be known to be mine, would oblige me to apply to myself those lines of the immortal John Milton, in one of his sonnets.

"I did but prompt the age to quit their cloggs
  By the plain rules of ancient Liberty,
  When lo! a barbarous noise surrounded me
  Of owls and cuckoos, asses, apes and dogs."[4]

Notes

1. Alexander Pope, *An Essay on Man,* Epistle III, lines 303–304.
2. All these men were heroes of the seventeenth-century English struggle against the tyranny, real or feared, of the Stuart kings James I, Charles I, Charles II, and James II. Algernon Sidney (1662–1683) was executed by the government of Charles II for having written (but not having published) *Discourses Concerning Government,* which was published after his death. John Harrington (1611–1677) wrote many works, in particular the utopian treatise *Oceana,* which sketched an ideal republican government. John Locke (1632–1704), the author

of the celebrated *Two Treatises of Government* and the *Essay Concerning Human Understanding,* was perhaps the greatest English philospher. Marchamont Nedham (1620–1678) wrote many republican works, including *The Excellence of a Free State.* Henry Neville (1620–1694) was a friend and ally of Harrington, and wrote *Plato Redividus.* Gilbert Burnet (1643–1715) was Bishop of Salisbury, an opponent of the Stuarts, and author of a famed history of England. Benjamin Hoadly (1675–1761), another adversary of the Stuarts, was later Bishop of Bangor, Hereford, Salisbury, and Winchester.

3. Alexander Pope, *An Essay on Man,* Epistle III, lines 19–20.

4. These lines are slightly misquoted from John Milton, "On the Detraction Which Followed Upon My Writing Certain Treatises," second part, "On the Same," lines 1–4. Besides being the author of the great epic poems *Paradise Lost, Paradise Regained,* and *Samson Agonistes,* Milton also supported the Puritan overthrow of Charles I and wrote many powerful and learned pamphlets supporting republican government for England.

Sources

ADAMS, CHARLES FRANCIS, ED., *The Works of John Adams,* 10 vols. Boston: Little, Brown, 1850–1856.

BUTTERFIELD, L. H., MARC FRIEDLANDER, AND MARY-JO KLINE, EDS., *The Book of Abigail and John: Selected Letters of the Adams Family, 1762–1784.* Cambridge, Mass.: Belknap Press of Harvard University Press, 1975.

BUTTERFIELD, L. H., ET AL., EDS., *The Diary and Autobiography of John Adams,* 4 vols. Cambridge, Mass.: Belknap Press of Harvard University Press, 1961.

CAPPON, LESTER J., ED., *The Adams-Jefferson Letters: The Complete Correspondence Between Thomas Jefferson and Abigail and John Adams,* 2 vols. Chapel Hill: University of North Carolina Press for the Institute of Early American History and Culture, 1959.

CAREY, GEORGE W., ED., *The Political Writings of John Adams.* Chicago: Regnery Publishing, Inc., 2000.

GELLES, EDITH B., *Portia: The World of Abigail Adams.* Bloomington: Indiana University Press, 1992.

HARASZTI, ZOLTAN, *John Adams and the Prophets of Progress.* Cambridge, Mass.: Harvard University Press, 1952.

LEVIN, PHYLLIS LEE, *Abigail Adams: A Biography.* New York: St. Martin's Press, 1987.

SCHUTZ, JOHN A., AND DOUGLASS G. ADAIR, EDS., *The Spur of Fame: Dialogues of John Adams and Benjamin Rush, 1805–1813.* San Marino, Calif.: Huntington Library, 1965; reprint ed., Indianapolis, Ind.: Liberty Fund, 2000.

SMITH, PAGE, *John Adams,* 2 vols. Garden City, N.Y.: Doubleday, 1962.

TAYLOR, ROBERT J., RICHARD RYERSON, ET AL., EDS., *The Papers of John Adams* (Cambridge, Mass.: Belknap Press of Harvard University Press, 1977–), 2: 284.

THOMPSON, C. BRADLEY, ED., *The Revolutionary Writings of John Adams.* Indianapolis, Ind.: Liberty Fund, 2000.

For Further Reading

Ferling, John E. *John Adams: A Life.* Knoxville: University of Tennessee Press, 1992; reprint ed., New York: Henry Holt, 1998.

Gelles, Edith B. *"First Thoughts": Life and Letters of Abigail Adams.* New York: Twayne Publishers, 1998.

Handler, Edward, *America and Europe in the Thought of John Adams.* Cambridge, Mass.: Harvard University Press, 1964.

Howe, John R., Jr., *The Changing Political Thought of John Adams.* Princeton, N.J.: Princeton University Press, 1965.

Shaw, Peter, *The Character of John Adams.* Chapel Hill: University of North Carolina Press for the Institute of Early American History and Culture, 1975.

Thompson, C. Bradley, *John Adams and the Spirit of Liberty*. Lawrence: University Press of Kansas, 1998.